a pinch of salt

Paul Jobin
a pinch of salt

Celebrating New Zealand food

Photography by Shaun Cato-Symonds

HarperCollins*Publishers*

I dedicate this cookbook to my beautiful
and very precious daughter, Cassandra.
I know my work in the hospitality industry
has made our times together challenging.
I look forward to her sharing this book
with her friends and future family.

National Library of New Zealand
Cataloguing-in-Publication Data

Jobin, Paul.
A Pinch of salt : celebrating New Zealand food / Paul Jobin.
Includes index.
ISBN 978-1-86950-760-2
1. Cookery, New Zealand. I. Title.
641.50993—dc 22

First published 2008
HarperCollins*Publishers (New Zealand) Limited*
P.O. Box 1, Auckland

ISBN 978 1 86950 760 2
Cover and internal design by IslandBridge
Food editor Pip Duncan
Printed by Bookbuilders, China on 128 gsm Matt Art

Contents

Acknowledgements

It is fair to say you can't publish a cookbook all on your lonesome. There are many individuals and companies who have supported me while I've been writing this cookbook and I sincerely thank them all. I'd especially like to thank:

Pip Duncan, my food editor, without whom this cookbook would never have happened. Pip is outstanding; the time she has given to this project, her energy, the use of her kitchen and her guidance is something to be applauded.

Shaun Cato-Symonds, whose magnificent photography first captured my work 11 years ago and now is here for us all to admire. I am truly grateful to him.

Chris and Leanne Chong at Red Cactus, fabulous mentors who encouraged me to tell my story throughout the book.

Bill Honeybone and Lorain Day at HarperCollins who believed in me right from the start and pushed me along to accomplish this feat, and Tracey Wogan and Eva Chan for pulling it all together.

My partner and best friend Lyndsay, who has supported me, been my harshest critic and been understanding in the times I disappeared to the 'cave' (office) for long periods of time.

Our children Cassandra, Emma and Joseph, who have shared this dream with me.

Close lifelong friends Darren and Linda, Richard and Christine, Warren and Vanessa, Esther and Coen, Sarah and Snow, Mal and Suzi, Vanessa and Richard, and Cricket and Con, who all have shared their ideas and encouragement through this project.

My parents, Roy and Dot Jobin, who backed me when many wouldn't have, and particular thanks to my father for his financial direction. I don't know if one lifetime is enough time to repay them.

All my Pure Tastes staff over the years who have put up with me being, at times, a focused, driven individual. Special thanks to Tobias Wilkinson, Chris Hagan and Carson Donaldson.

My talented friends in hospitality who have chewed my ear and all deserve to share their culinary ideas with you too: Neil Brazier, Brenton Low, Hughie Blues, Michael Meredith, Chris Harris, Brent and Carol Cameron, Sam Timoko, Andrew Brown, David Griffiths, Cameron Lawless, Jason Dell and Natasha MacAller.

The businesses that have backed my work and created opportunities for me: Catherine Bell at *Dish* magazine; Michael Barker and Nicky Sheed at Barker's Fruit Processors; Rod Slater, Tanya Hart and Jennie Dean at Beef and Lamb New Zealand; Stephen Gibson at New Zealand King Salmon; Ivan, Vivienne, Lynette, Colin, Dick and Marilyn at First Drop Olive Oil; Rhona and Marcel at Lemon Fresh; Jo Bates at *Taste* magazine; Kate King and Alison McKee at Gourmet Direct; Tony Gibbs at Turners and Growers; Tony Taylor at Wholesale Produce Company; Noel, Ian, Judi and our students at the Culinary Institute of New Zealand and Ray Vail at Domestic Agencies for the beautiful crockery used in the shoots.

The following food purveyors, who embraced the cookbook and allowed Shaun to photograph me in their very busy premises: Zarbo Delicatessen and Cafe, Newmarket; Mahadeo's Spice, Dhal and Produce Warehouse, Mt Eden; Silver Bell Market, Mt Eden; Auckland Fish Market, Auckland City; and Monsoon Poon Restaurant, Auckland City.

The team at Eyeworks TV: Carlenna, my first director, who had to show me the ropes of talking to camera, and Kari, my present director, who keeps my nose pointed forward with care. Julia Bayliss and the rest of the team at the Living Channel and my incredible host, the lovely April Ieremia.

Finally, I wish to thank certain foodies who believed in my cooking, understood how I ticked and encouraged me along: Mike and Janneke; Mary and Dan; Marcel and Rhona; Lyn Barnes; Annette and Neil Plowman; Ruth Marinier; Colleen and Walter; Terry Faith Weihs; Pete, Tissi, Brenda and Steve and many others.

And thanks to you, the reader. I hope you enjoy cooking from this book. Remember, the wonderful thing about the art of cooking is that you are always evolving, learning new ideas and flavours, improving the ones you know already and understanding that all the cuisines around the world are there to be enjoyed.

Foreword

by April Ieremia
Television presenter,
April in the Afternoon

In this day and age where it's fashionable for TV chefs to be precious, arrogant or downright rude, Paul Jobin is an exception. Not only is he one of the finest chefs to come from New Zealand but without a doubt he is also one of the nicest.

Born in Whakatane, Paul's love of cooking began, like most, at his grandmother's apron strings around the age of eight.

Now with 22 years of expertise under his toque, Paul has been part of renowned culinary teams around the world as well as at two of New Zealand's most luxurious resorts, Huka Lodge in Taupo and The Lodge at Kauri Cliffs in Northland. Showcasing his cooking talents in cities as diverse as Sydney, Bratislava, Prague and New York demonstrates the world-class quality of his work.

These days, armed with a Japanese knife and a microplane, Paul promises to tantalise our tastebuds with recipes that are not only easy on the palate but are without a doubt visual symphonies.

I recently had the pleasure of working with this fine chef when the 41-year-old became a regular fixture on my show, *April in the Afternoon*. Paul's boundless enthusiasm and ability inspire someone like me, who failed Cooking 101, to attempt his gastronomic masterpieces. His endearing humour, extensive knowledge and passion for food are infectious and have propelled me to a new area of interest.

As a result, I have impressed friends with dishes such as salmon, cucumber tzatziki and orange gremolata. I have achieved simple mastery in cooking the perfect poached egg and when it comes to dessert, turning out mouth-watering calorie-loaded chocolate tarts is now a specialty.

Over the years, Paul's television experience has included guest appearances on shows such as TV One's *Good Morning*, the *Taste New Zealand Christmas Special*, Food TV's *New Zealand on a Plate* and *Master Class* before becoming a Master Chef on *April in the Afternoon*.

Now, after a few months working on the show, Paul's quiet and unassuming manner has flourished with his growing confidence. The charming and engaging relationship he has developed with the camera has led to a more than favourable response from our viewers, complimenting him not only on his recipes but also his relaxed style.

However, it was an invitation to join the staff of a restaurant in England with three Michelin stars that truly reflects his talent and the respect in which he is held in the industry. Paul chose to stay in New Zealand, cooking modern global food inspired by his extensive globetrotting and breathtaking local experiences.

Paul is a treasure and I wish him all the very best with his first book on his first love.

Foreword

by Catherine Bell
Editorial director,
Dish magazine

When I established The Epicurean Workshop and its associated cooking school in 1989 I had several aims, one of which was to give a platform to chefs, both well known and unknown.

One of the up-and-coming young chefs I got to know was Paul Jobin. My first encounter with Paul came when I sponsored and judged a category at the annual Salon Culinaire competitions in the early nineties. I noticed him because he won — his dish, a hot dessert, stood out far and away ahead of the other contestants.

Later he came to my attention again when people started to tell me about the fantastic food a young chef was serving at a restaurant in Tairua. I immediately invited him to teach at Epicurean, although by the time his class was scheduled he was fortuitously back in Auckland at Paramount. Everyone who came was blown away by his food, a skilful fusion of Asian and Western ingredients, beautifully presented on the plate.

Paul showcased his food at Epicurean several times over the years that followed, by then as executive chef at the acclaimed Lodge at Kauri Cliffs. He was a pleasure to host as his recipes always arrived on time, with *mise en place* lists, equipment lists and even suppliers' names and contacts should we need them. This was rarely the case with most guest chefs!

In the ensuing years he became one of the country's chefs to watch and now he has a high and respected profile amongst his peers and the dining public. It amazes me how he fits all that he does — consulting, tutoring, writing, television, demonstrations and more — into his life.

This book is a testament to his hard work and his enduring talent as a fine chef. But what pleases me most is that *A Pinch of Salt* is aimed at people who cook at home. It is not simply a showcase of his most challenging dishes. Not every chef can relate to home cooking, but Paul has made sure the recipes work well in a home kitchen. Head notes that contain useful information about ingredients sit alongside tales of kitchen experiences that have influenced him throughout his life. This is a book that is designed to inspire and definitely one that should be cooked from often. Congratulations.

We spend half our lives working, trying to establish a career that in later years sets us up to enjoy retirement and the fruits of our hard work. Anyone who knows me well will tell you that I am a very focused, motivated and passionate individual who sets out to do the best I can in the lifetime I have. I have always believed that my achievements will be best shared with my future grandchildren, teaching them to apply themselves, to be focused and to strive to be the best they can. Some people believe that because they are talented, opportunities will come knocking at their door. To me they live only in hope; the reality is that you have to make the effort and chase your goals. Completing this cookbook has always been a priority in my career. I am proud to share my culinary journey, which at times has been both tough and inspiring. I share our antipodean way of cooking, in fantastic recipes that have been used time and time again, recipes which are flavour-driven and embrace freshly grown produce. I share professional cooking secrets, glimpses into the life of a chef and challenges I have faced.

My intention is to excite you into trying new dishes.

My belief is that we should all have an open mind about food. No single cuisine is 'the best'. If you are in the restaurant scene, you don't need to have a Michelin star to be considered a great chef. When I get the chance, I love to travel, and I am always stimulated by the variety of different ingredients and techniques I discover. When cooking, I look first for seasonal produce, locally grown, and allow that to inspire the dish I create. Ingredients should have a purpose on a plate, and not be there just because they sound good or trendy. Flavours must sing out and be noticed, textures discovered and healthy eating embraced.

'A pinch of salt' is the way we bring out the flavour in food. If we season food correctly, we don't even need to put salt on the table. How many people do you know who salt their food at the dining table before they have even tried their meal? I consider pepper a spice, to be added only when the dish actually needs it. Pepper is great freshly milled over pasta or risotto but how many restaurants bring out a pepper grinder — sometimes as long as a softball bat — to mill over your red Thai prawn curry?

To understand the food combinations in this cookbook, you need to know a little about me. My fascination with food started when I least expected it. During the school holidays, I would stay with my Kiwi grandparents in Whakatane, Bay of Plenty. My grandparents had a huge vegetable garden surrounded by fruit trees. My grandfather would get up early in the morning to split firewood, and I would stack and trundle the kindling into the house for Grandma's wood-fired range. Grandma would discuss what she wanted to cook for lunch and dinner, and we would gather the vegetables and berries needed. Looking back, I appreciated the time I spent cooking with her, shelling peas, making preserves and jams, making bread and baking goodies that went into metal Griffins tins. Recently, it has been good to see these old-world skills coming back in great cafés around New Zealand. Grandma's plum, rhubarb and cinnamon crumble was legendary; she would send me out into the backyard to get plums from the tree. Two hours later, she would come looking for me when I failed to return. She usually found me quietly eating away in the plum tree with plum stones all over the ground.

Other times, I would stay with my English nana in Mission Bay, Auckland. Her traditional cooking was quite the opposite of Grandma's. Dainty little tea cakes served on a high-tea stand and finger sandwiches with the crust perfectly cut off. Here I learnt to make a great scone, Yorkshire pudding, toad in the hole, and sherry trifle — great English classics. My grandfather would make up mathematics test papers for my brother and me, and every question right won us 50 cents. Those maths drills later helped me to understand costings in my profession. Money well earned, we treated ourselves to a bus ride into the city to watch *Gumball Rally* and *E.T.* for the fourth time — I loved that movie!

After school, I worked as a porter in Johnsonville, Wellington, at a mid-range hotel. I had hoped to join the airforce as a catering cadet when I left school, but their intake was full. Instead I asked at the hotel about an apprenticeship. I had a trial with the chef at the time, a big bellowing man. I learned how to cook my first steak: if the customer sent it back and asked for it well done, we would put it on a solid-top electric hob, place a 15-litre stockpot on top and cook it again for three minutes flat. Talk about a 'Dunlop retread'!

One day I went to work and the chef had left; my new head chef was a little Japanese man, Takashi Shigeeda. He didn't think much of apprentices at the time. I beavered away working six days a week as a kitchenhand, keeping my mouth shut and my pencil busy. During my time at the hotel, a Russian cruise liner sank in the Picton Channel. Wellington hotels all had to accommodate some of the ship's rescued crew, and our hotel hosted the cooks and stewards. Ivan, a Hungarian chef on our staff, was put in charge of cooking for the Russians. He made fish broth the colour of tomatoes, so hot the guests were breaking into a sweat. The next day we crumbed little pieces of fish, all 20kg of it, and Ivan made special fish cakes that he claimed the Russians loved, from the leftover glug of beaten egg and crumbs from the coating mixture. The guests consumed the fish cakes, uncooked in the centre, remains hanging from the men's moustaches.

When it was time to leave this hotel, I received my first lesson in how staff celebrate when a fellow staff member leaves an establishment in the hospitality industry. My farewell gift wasn't apparent at first. My colleagues had unscrewed the shower rose, placed dye capsules in it and waited for me to have a shower at the end of a hard day. I came out looking like a tri-coloured Popsicle!

Takashi had opened Wellington's first Japanese restaurant and he felt it was time for me to step up to cooking. I was also studying part-time at Wellington Polytechnic (Weltec) for my London City and Guilds. My training at Akiyoshi was the best way for me to learn, even though as a 19-year-old I may not have seen it that way. I had to clean and polish the chefs' shoes, arranging them side by side at the door; sharpen the sashimi knives; make the tempura batter; and when the chef arrived, have a pot of green tea at the ready. My day would then start.

At the end of the evening the small staff of the 35-seater restaurant would assemble for dinner, among the pots of incredible smells, sashimi, shiitake tempura and sushi. During my first month, I was given a bowl of peas and some long chopsticks and I had to pick up each pea with my chopsticks before I was allowed to tuck into dinner. In their special way, they were training me to cook with chopsticks. Most apprentices started with metal tongs, but not me. With the additional karate training from black-belt Takashi on my day off, I came to understand how to be focused, true to myself, respectful and self-analysing. I use all of these skills today in both my professional and personal life. Takashi was the best mentor and provided a great start for a lad like me. I will always be grateful for his guidance.

I left Akiyoshi in order to learn another food style and also finish my qualifications fulltime. I joined a modern French-inspired restaurant, Plimmer House, during the nouvelle cuisine era. Nouvelle cuisine has always had a bad rap, often described as tiny portions of food at huge prices with diners needing to grab some takeaways on the way home. That was the downside, sure, but the nouvelle cuisine trend also brought us colourful presentation, more use of fresh produce, lighter food and made us consider healthier cooking options, such as removing the roux and reducing the captured flavour. Food processors, nonstick pans, blenders and portable steamers all made their mark during this time.

At Plimmer House I was privileged to work with two head chefs, Paul Hoather and Mark Limacher. They were both talented in their own right, yet so different in their approach to food, and were influenced by world-renowned chefs Freddy Girardet and Joël Robuchon. Paul was exceptionally talented in plate composition and Mark's insight was the extraction of flavour that is a hallmark of a great chef. This was where I now started to concentrate my efforts.

Mark once made a simple green salad for a tasting menu. Several salad leaves were picked, washed and lightly spun dry. The ends of the lettuce leaves were dipped in flavoured oils such as hazelnut and walnut. The salad dressing was made and chilled to an emulsion. The dressing was placed in the middle of blanched butterhead leaves, which were then folded and placed in the centre of the salad greens. Mark loved the mystery element in food, catching the diners by surprise as they pierced the salad packet and self-dressed the salad as they ate — brilliant!

I moved on from Plimmer House to try my hand at running my first kitchen at a dine-and-dance venue in Whitby. I ended up doing 70-hour weeks, and some weeks my wage cheque bounced. I was very naïve, and decided to move to Auckland to work as a larder chef for a load less money but far more opportunity to learn. My Japanese training had taught me to make dressings and broths but I needed to work on making sauces, so I asked Norman Arents at Prickly Pear restaurant for a position. Norman was an amazing chef, very fast and skilled. His restaurant was almost always fully booked and awards adorned his walls. Within seven months I had moved from larder chef past our chef de partie to sous chef. It wasn't unusual to be on edge during service: a plate of pumpkin gnocchi and smoked chicken might come flying — I would duck and a bomb scene would be created all over the wall. Among the broken glass plate-warmer doors and recurring frowns, I built a strong relationship with Norman and he made me a more technically sound chef.

During this time, I lived a 35-minute cycle ride from the restaurant. One particular day, I didn't have to start at the restaurant until 2 p.m. so I decided to make some chilli oil. Running late for work, I went to the toilet without first washing my hands. Riding my bike up the hill, I had become so hot around the nether regions that I could no longer sit on the seat; hell, I was on fire below. I had to negotiate intersections regardless of the traffic signals, with motorists looking on in amazement as a toxic-looking cyclist zoomed past. I had ridden to work in 25 minutes! Surely this must be the best way for Cycling New Zealand to achieve gold at competition events.

Overseas beckoned, so I went off to Sydney, Australia. A sous chef position had been organised for me in a 30-year-old restaurant in Surry Hills. I learned a lot of lessons here, including that different countries have different names for the same ingredients. I ordered spinach and got silverbeet (I should have asked for English spinach), ordered shallots and got spring onions (I should have asked for eschallots). I lived down the road from the restaurant, and it wasn't uncommon for staff to bang on my front door and tell me I had to work because there were 180 diners booked and half the cooks hadn't turned up for work. It became a lot harder after the other sous chef had a heart attack and management sacked the head chef without informing me. Great, all on my own with two apprentices and a prep hand! Who am I, Houdini?

I needed stimulus from more experienced chefs, real operations and food that had meaning. So I saved up and ate out whenever I could, and also worked at éstages for free where I learned a lot and was motivated. The Australian scene has some of the best food in the world with innovative chefs not afraid to challenge culinary boundaries. Because of Australia's multicultural society, the French influence has lessened and food has become simpler on the plate. The ingredients are excellent quality and are fused together for a reason. I discovered a chef who had just started his own restaurant. I loved his food; it was like no other in Sydney at the time. I would return to my head chef position at the Kirk on Crown, Darlinghurst, and rave about this chef. My staff thought I was on another planet but I knew he was destined to become a star. Today Tetsuya Wakuda is acclaimed throughout the world, known for both his palate and technique.

An Australian chef and I were offered a two-month contract to cook in Bratislava, Slovakia. Our wages were to be paid in two instalments, one half into my bank account at home and the other half in Slovak currency. We spent a few days cooking in Rome, Milan and Vienna, which was not long enough and where I want to return one day. We were picked up by our host and a translator who looked like the ultimate front-row prop for the All Blacks, and driven across the Danube River into Bratislava.

We were asked to run the restaurant and showcase antipodean food techniques. On our first night we were taken for the best pizza in town — the pizzas were inverted with the mozzarella cheese on the base, then the filling and the tomato sauce on top — my God, what a disaster! So we made pizza the right way and put it on the lunch menu, and what a stir we caused. One day, as we were showing staff how to make fresh pasta and hang it over broom handles to dry, a waiter offered me a cappuccino. It was at this precise moment that I realised just how different the food is in Eastern Europe. My cappuccino was made with dark Turkish coffee and condensed milk.

Our hulking translator also happened to be our bodyguard. We discovered this when we were chased around the city by Hungarian gypsies, paid to knock us off because we had taken business away from other restaurants. After this adventure we were whisked away to the mountains for three days to cook in the villages, away from all the commotion. We were asked to extend our contract for two years but who was going to stay around and live a life like that? So we went to Prague and cooked in a restaurant that catered for the film crew of *Mission Impossible* for four days. I returned home and am still owed wages from the Bratislava contract as none of my Australian wages had been banked. Another huge lesson learned.

Before leaving Sydney for Bratislava I had accepted a position at Huka Lodge, near Taupo. My time there with chef Greg Heffernan was invaluable. Here I relearned the classic French cooking techniques. Greg's kitchen was well oiled, sound, organised and disciplined. Some of the names to have trained under Greg include Stephen Morris and Rex Morgan. My time at Huka Lodge was a huge learning curve, both professionally and personally. Greg's influence and mentoring has helped me to become stronger in all areas of my career.

Since then I have had positions in various restaurants; chefs are very transient people. At Shells Restaurant in Tairua, Coromandel Peninsula, I worked as head chef for Martin and Kay Van Lubeck. This was the first time I was chosen as a finalist for the Cervena Plates competition and a Beef and Lamb Hallmarks of Excellence Ambassador. Winning these awards helped me enormously and my profile started to grow. I became co-head chef and then head chef at Paramount Restaurant, Auckland, owned by Shaun Smith. This gave me the platform to really showcase my passion and my unique food style. Here I was lucky to make friendships with talented individuals such as David Griffiths, Nicolas Huffman, Simon and Creghan Wright and quiet achiever Michael Meredith. I received awards for my famous black lacquer duck and won the prestigious 1999 Metro Restaurant of the Year award.

During this time, my daughter Cassandra, now a little foodie in her own right, came into my life. The biggest parenting mistake I made was feeding her large amounts of fresh asparagus at two years of age. Now 10, she can't stand the stuff; if I wave a spear I get a creased forehead and a stern stare! I have my food hates too; family and close friends love to wind me up by offering me cans of baked beans or canned tuna. And at bring-a-plate parties I always cringe when I see the worst Kiwi canapé ever: canned asparagus rolls. Yuck!

Julian and Josie Robertson ate regularly at Paramount and were about to open The Lodge at Kauri Cliffs on a PGA-standard golf course in Matauri Bay, Northland. They hired me as their executive chef. This was endorsed by Hendrik Wassenaar, with whom I had worked at Huka Lodge. The Lodge at Kauri Cliffs was not quite finished, so I was flown to New York to work for the Robertsons alongside their fantastic chef Trudy Ainge. Each morning we would go out into Manhattan and purchase our ingredients for dinner, each night a different menu. Here I discovered fresh ceps (porcini mushrooms), morels, Arctic char fish, squid with tentacles (I had only ever worked with squid tubes), fresh shiso (green perilla) and pomegranates.

I also learned that Americans like snappy service, no waiting please! I remember making a lemon-curd soufflé where the curd was poured like molten lava into the soufflé. A soufflé takes 15 minutes and I was still getting used to Fahrenheit oven temperatures. After five minutes of waiting for dessert, Julian asked me about the delay and said it was ridiculous to create a dessert that would take that long to prepare. I was shattered; this dessert was the pinnacle of my cooking.

I had a chance to cook at the Robertsons' private residence on Long Island. Fate often directs our future, and in this case I was given a mountain bike to ride into Oyster Cove. I was hungry, and stopped at a corner store to get a sandwich and a soda. They started to 'build' the sandwich: orange-coloured cheese, sliced square ham, sauerkraut and American mustard all wrapped with wax paper in a brown paper bag. I experienced a *Forrest Gump* moment, exiting the store, unwrapping the sandwich, and staring at it in awe, so fat and high I wondered how to fit it into my mouth. I headed back to New Zealand, not knowing this experience would save my kitchen an embarrassing moment.

The Lodge at Kauri Cliffs opened on Christmas Eve, not exactly a great time for a restaurant as New Zealand all but stops around this time. As a chef you have to hope you have enough provisions to see you through the Christmas–

New Year break. We were making up to 60 sandwiches a day for the golfers. A waiter came rushing into the kitchen, knees quivering, complaining about a guest who had 'had a gutsful' of New Zealand sandwiches. They were made with exotic ingredients and strange pickles! I met with the guest, who launched into a full-on explanation of how sandwiches should be made. He was American so I asked him to give me the benefit of the doubt and allow me to make what he had just described. I retreated back to my domain, the staff in the kitchen quiet, and I visualised the sandwich I had eaten on the park bench. I started to build him this monstrosity of a sandwich. I didn't have any sauerkraut so I mixed a little vinegar into our caramelised onions. I wrapped it in wax paper and took it out to him. The moment of truth: he took a bite, a smile beamed across his face, he hugged me and said, 'There is a god, a chef who can make a sandwich. Hallelujah!'

I met Michael Campbell, New Zealand's No. 1 PGA golfer at the time, a fantastic bloke, very calm and a bit of a foodie. He asked if I could make him a chicken salad with spinach and said that he loved calamari. I set about marinating the squid in puréed kiwifruit, no longer than 10 minutes otherwise the squid tenderizes and becomes a purée too. I sent the dish out, he raved, it's a hit! Michael requested kiwifruit calamari, polenta chips and avocado salad for guests he had joining him for a late dinner. We included the dish on our à la carte menu. That night the waitstaff enthusiastically told the early diners about the legend behind this dish, and we sold out. There wasn't a sliver of squid in the building and Michael hadn't dined yet! I had to decide whether to have the waitstaff peel shallots for four days or to run for my life. Michael came into the kitchen: 'Hey Paul, I've spent all day talking this dish up with my buddies on the golf course. Tell me you're joking that there's no more left?' I swallowed hard, and wanted to bury my maitre d' in the squid cartons piled up in the dockway. I had to snake my way out by driving to the supermarket 35kms away to buy more squid to serve him for lunch the next day.

Following that season, I decided I had done my time; four-and-a-half years was a good innings for a chef not always able to write his own menu. I missed cooking overseas and was hoping to secure a position at Tetsuya's, in Sydney. Brenton Low, who is a good friend and a talented chef with A Deco restaurant, Whangarei, talked me out of it and suggested that it was time I had a crack at running my own restaurant.

During my time at The Lodge at Kauri Cliffs, my then-wife and I operated Pure Tastes, a cooking school that travelled all over Northland. We were New Zealand's only mobile cooking school, holding themed classes at private locations with our trailer full of barstools and bins of equipment. Attendees at the classes suggested it was time for Kerikeri to have a high-end restaurant. So Pure Tastes the restaurant was born.

I was now a single man; the hospitality industry is really tough on any serious relationship. I had enough savings from holiday pay to see me through till the restaurant opened, but that was all. I turned to my father, Roy, and asked him if he would provide funds to get me started. It was a tough decision for him; he was a credit lending manager for ANZ Bank, and hospitality as a rule wasn't a bank's best bet for lending money. A great proportion of restaurants don't make it past 18 months; if they can stay in business for three years or more then they are more likely to succeed. On the other hand, he could see his son needed a chance to prove himself, to earn his stripes and that he was talented enough to succeed.

Pure Tastes opened in a side street next to a gym in September 2004. As with any new restaurant, you get your honeymoon period, and then everyone becomes a food critic. During the year I realised Northland had very abrupt tourism seasons. If the All Blacks were playing, the restaurant would be dead! The side street we were in wasn't the best location, and the numbers having lunch each day varied so much it was difficult to roster staff. It was a nightmare! There was talk around town that some thought Kerikeri didn't need a 'city' restaurant, because our prices were higher than others. This really agitated me because we were going to the trouble of making our own pasta or gnocchi dough, filled with goat's cheese or local organic aged gouda, our own smoked duck-leg meat with a mushroom foam and lemon oil, all for only two dollars more! I quickly realised that we weren't going to make it unless I changed the marketing of Pure Tastes to promote it as a dining destination for visitors to the Bay of Islands.

During this time I had a call from Ray Arnesen, asking me to consider moving Pure Tastes to his hotel, Paihia Beach Resort and Spa. In December 2005 we moved the chattels and staff to the coastal town 25 minutes east of Kerikeri. Our summer tourism window of operation was longer than in Kerikeri but the winter months were tougher. Kerikeri diners tended to support local restaurants in the winter, whereas Paihia and Russell locals preferred to hibernate or travel to warmer destinations.

My own portfolio of activities was changing; I was doing more outside catering, more demonstrations such as at the Ellerslie International Flower Show, more industry-based guest chef dinners, and development work with Barker's Fruit Processors and other private companies wanting a leading edge in their food products. My staff had doubled to cover three meals each day, seven days a week, a big step up from the old Pure Tastes where we were closed Sundays and didn't do Saturday lunch. My health began to deteriorate, and I would puff frantically when exercising or doing a busy service in the kitchen. My doctor organised an appointment for a CT scan at Whangarei hospital, where I was quickly admitted to the emergency department. I had a rather large blood clot above my lung; luckily it stayed there and decided not to travel to my heart. The head nurse told me that if it had been left untreated for three more days I would have been a dead man. This really made me stop and push replay; I had to get a fix on where I was at with this business. I decided to work through the summer and see how I coped as we headed into winter 2007. I was OK, but found it was taking longer to recover from long hours on my feet in the kitchen. I let my business partner know I would like to move on.

During 2007 my profile gathered momentum; all the hard yards were starting to pay off. I was now learning about how to cook on television, winning business awards and being offered interesting jobs. In our second year at the Ellerslie International Flower Show, we performed a really show-stopping, entertaining cooking demonstration with the backing of Fisher & Paykel appliances. It was during this time I started to write this cookbook, and I was lucky enough to have a strong kitchen crew led by Tobias Wilkinson, who worked with me 11 years ago at Paramount and who, incidentally, helped me with the photography in this book.

Today, I have a part-time role tutoring at the local hospitality training school, the Culinary Institute of New Zealand. I am proud to be a part of this Institute. The tutors, led by Noel McRae, are passionate and take the trainees (commis) way past what they need to learn to get their qualifications. I have a lot more freedom now to concentrate on my ongoing television work (*April in the Afternoon* and *New Zealand on a Plate*) and developing great new products for Barker's and others.

This cookbook is a lifelong dream. The recipes are alive, are designed to inspire and taste fantastic. It's a book I want you to use in the kitchen, not leave to sit unopened on the coffee table or in the bookshelf for too long. Some recipes may seem long, but you don't have to cook the whole thing. Try one of the components and introduce it to your meal. And above all, keep an open mind to food. Challenge at times why certain flavours can or can't go together; support your local talented restaurant chefs; and if you have a local farmers' market, make it a part of your family life, for there is nothing better than cooking with fresh ingredients.

Paul Jobin
Kerikeri, 2008

Signature
dishes

Good chefs with a bit of mileage under their belt find a
handful of dishes over time that are so fine-tuned they
no longer need refining. This special collection is known
as signature dishes and diners will make frequent visits
to a restaurant as long as the signature dish is available. I
am proud to include these three as some of my signature
dishes; they are all-time favourites with family, friends and
customers alike.

Below

Scandinavian cured salmon   page 60

Right above

Sweet Thai crispy beef and coconut rice   page 82

Right below

Quivering white chocolate tart   page 97

Culinary birds

I find chicken versatile and easy to cook, and it works well with many other ingredients. Many New Zealanders think so too — over the last 20 years, our poultry consumption has more than doubled. We now eat our way through nearly 150,000 tonnes a year of this great-tasting, lean source of protein.

I must say, however, that my favourite culinary bird is duck. If I am dining out and duck is on the menu, I feel obliged to order it. The flavour is fantastic, the skin when crisped is delectable. I recall demonstrating Chinese duck with squid dumplings to a cooking class when a regular diner from Paramount days announced to the room: 'I can personally vouch that Paul is Auckland's top duck chef. I've tried every duck dish he has done!' From then on my duck sales tripled — so much so that I once cleaned out Auckland's duck-leg supplies. The Pekin is the only commercial duck breed available in New Zealand.

In my days at Kauri Cliffs my kitchen crew started to acquire some Michelin-star muscle. We used a technique for roasting chicken breast often found in British restaurants. The chicken is roasted on its frame and when done, the chef places a metal skewer in the chicken breast and then on their lip to see how hot it is. Once the required temperature is met, the breast is deboned and the chicken returned to the oven to finish the legs. The frame is then chopped into pieces and used to make a sauce. Like meat roasts, birds cooked on the bone just taste so much better.

Dukkah chicken, pear, feta and spinach salad

Serves 4

¼ cup	indigenous dukkah (see page 92)
12	chicken tenderloins
3 tablespoons	olive oil
28	large spinach leaves, stems removed
1	pear, sliced thinly
200g	goat feta, crumbled
1 cup	tomato lemon vinaigrette (see page 68)

Tip the dukkah onto a dinner plate.

Coat the chicken tenderloins in the dukkah.

Moderately heat a sauté pan, add the olive oil and chicken and sauté both sides until golden.

Shred the spinach leaves into a mixing bowl. Add the pear, feta and a little of the vinaigrette. Slice the chicken and place on a plate, drizzle with a little vinaigrette, top with some salad, repeat, dress with the remaining vinaigrette and serve.

Michael Campbell, New Zealand's top golfer at the time, was staying at Kauri Cliffs while training for the New Zealand Open. He needed a bit of a boost to get him through the afternoon, so I made this dish for his lunch; not only did he devour it but it also became a hit with the resort's predominantly American clientele who love healthy fat-free food. I featured this recipe when I was cooking on the Living Channel show *April in the Afternoon*. The ingredients are easy to obtain and quick to prepare — sounds like heaven, doesn't it?

Five-spice quail, apple persimmon slaw and honey

Serves 4

I just have to include my favourite quail recipe in this cookbook. Quail is a very small and tasty bird, and one I wish more people ordered in restaurants. I was once a chef in an 80-seat brasserie in St Heliers on the Auckland waterfront where I had two kitchenhands from Shanghai. They introduced me to making dim sums and cooking birds in master stock (stock flavoured with soy, maltose and red vinegar); in turn, I taught them how to make fresh pasta. This dish is worth the effort; the aromatic smells are sensational and the taste sublime!

Five-spice quail

2 litres	chicken stock
½ cup	dark soy sauce
4	garlic cloves, smashed
1 knob	ginger, grated
4	spring onions, chopped
4	quails, patted dry with paper towels, wishbone removed
4 teaspoons	Chinese five-spice powder
2 teaspoons	Sichuan pepper (alternatively pink peppercorns)
4 tablespoons	sea salt

In a large saucepan, bring the chicken stock, soy sauce, garlic, ginger and spring onions to the boil.

Plunge the quail into the stock and blanch for 2 minutes.

Take out the quail, remove the breasts, placing the legs and frame back into the stock for a further 5 minutes or until cooked. Take out of the stock and bone the legs from the frame.

Meanwhile, mix the Chinese five-spice powder, Sichuan pepper and sea salt together in a small bowl.

Apple persimmon slaw

¼	crisp green cabbage, finely shredded, stored in chilled water
½	red onion, thinly sliced and stored in chilled water
1	Jazz apple, julienned
1	persimmon, peeled and sliced thinly
¼ cup	currants, soaked in jasmine tea till plump, then drained
3 tablespoons	chopped coriander
3 tablespoons	chopped mint
1	lemon, zested and juiced
1 cup	mayonnaise
¾ cup	rice vinegar
½ cup	Shaoxing rice vinegar (or ⅓ cup malt vinegar)
125g	liquid honey

Preheat the oven to 195°C.

Place the cabbage and red onion in a salad spinner and spin dry.

In a mixing bowl, toss together the cabbage, onion, apple, persimmon, currants, coriander and mint.

In a separate bowl, whisk together the lemon zest, juice and mayonnaise.

In a saucepan, bring the vinegars and honey to the boil, simmer, reducing the syrup to a thickish consistency.

Line a baking tray with nonstick paper, place the quail breast and legs on the paper and drizzle over the honey vinegar syrup.

Season with the five-spice salt and roast in the oven till golden and aromatic (about 5–7 minutes).

Meanwhile, mix the slaw with the mayonnaise and place a spoonful onto the plate.

Place the quail on top and drizzle a little more of the honey vinegar over the dish.

Crispy duck salad

Serves 6

Roast duck

1 teaspoon	cardamom seeds, ground
1 teaspoon	star anise, ground
1 teaspoon	cloves, ground
1 teaspoon	cinnamon, ground
1 teaspoon	coriander seeds, ground
1 teaspoon	ginger powder
1 tablespoon	sea salt
6	duck breasts
2 tablespoons	grapeseed oil

In a mixing bowl, place the first six spice ingredients and mix well together.

Diagonally score the skin of the breasts 1cm apart. Season the duck breasts all over with the spices and salt.

On a low–medium heat, heat the oil in a sauté pan; add the duck breasts skin side down.

Roast the duck breast in the pan on the skin (about 4 minutes). The skin will render and melt as the breast cooks which will protect the duck from overcooking.

Flip the duck breast over and seal the flesh; remove from the pan and rest on a cooling rack. Reserve the juices from the roasting pan for the salad.

Slice the duck into thin pieces on an angle.

Salad

¼ cup	red wine vinegar
¼ cup	apple juice
2 teaspoons	American mustard
	the reserved duck juices from the roasting pan (not the fat)
1 tablespoon	liquid honey
½ cup	extra virgin olive oil
2	heads cos lettuce (romaine), washed
200g	rocket (arugula) leaves
1	green mango, julienned
2	avocados, peeled and diced
1 cup	cashews or walnuts, toasted

Whisk together the red wine vinegar, apple juice, American mustard, duck roasting juices and honey. While whisking, gradually drizzle in the extra virgin olive oil.

In a large mixing bowl, briefly toss together the cos, rocket, mango, avocado, cashews or walnuts and duck.

Toss the salad together with some of the vinaigrette and serve with a glass of chilled pinot gris.

While working in Sydney it wasn't uncommon for me to go to BBQ King in Chinatown to buy a Peking duck to take home, shred the meat and make this salad. It is a winner of a salad and one I couldn't take off our menu in the restaurant for over four menu changes. Even when it wasn't in print, our regulars still ordered it. This salad illustrates my philosophy that food should be fresh, zingy and textural. You won't be disappointed . . .

Phuket chicken larb

Serves 10–12

Curry paste

15 peeled shallots, finely sliced

15 garlic cloves, peeled and finely sliced

4 coriander roots and stems, chopped

4 chillies, oiled and blackened all over in a sauté pan and peeled

10 white peppercorns, soaked in cold water and drained

Place the shallots, garlic, coriander and chillies in a pestle and mortar or a food processor. Pound or blend until well crushed. Add in the white peppercorns and continue to blend until smooth.

I discovered this wonderful dish of spiced mince wrapped in a lettuce cup when we stopped for dinner on James Bond Island, after our kayak trip through the Phang Nga Bay limestone caves in Phuket, Thailand. This fast, aromatic dish is fantastic served as finger food, a late-afternoon snack or a serious starter to a dinner on the deck with ice-cold New Zealand sparkling mineral water.

Chicken mince is relatively inexpensive to purchase and must be freshly minced so that the fried flavours stand out, refresh the palate and kick you into gear!

Larb

½ cup vegetable oil

2 x 400ml cans coconut cream

4 Kaffir lime leaves, julienned

curry paste (see recipe at left)

1kg chicken mince

¾ cup palm sugar or raw sugar

2 tablespoons fish sauce

4 tablespoons lime juice

1 cup basil leaves, julienned

1 cup cashew nuts, roasted and crushed

¼ iceburg lettuce shredded finely

20 square rice paper sheets

In a large wok or heavy-bottomed saucepan, heat the vegetable oil until smoking hot.

Add the coconut cream (which will splatter), the Kaffir lime leaves and the curry paste, and reduce until it starts to split (about 7 minutes). Add the mince and fry in the coconut cream until well browned (about a further 8 minutes). Add the palm sugar and mix well. Add in the fish sauce and lime juice. Fold in the basil and cashew nuts. Remove from the heat and pour onto a tray to cool down.

Half fill a container with hot water. Dip the rice paper in the water till limp; place on a damp tea towel in a diamond shape. On the corner closest to you, place a spoonful of larb onto the rice paper and top with some of the lettuce. Start to roll the wrapper then fold in the sides and continue to roll into a cigar shape.

To store, place on a damp tea towel, cover and refrigerate until required.

Earthly treasures

The rich volcanic soils around New Zealand nurture some amazing vegetables. These include the humble potato that is such a part of our everyday lives; the orange kumara, all smoky and sweet, cooked in baskets in the Maori hangi; the Ohakune carrots grown below the glistening ski fields of Tongariro National Park; and the famous Pukekohe Longkeeper onions harvested in the Bombay Hills south of Auckland. We have all grown up with these vegetables, which become our staple diet in the cold winter months when we're snuggled in front of the fire, pillow on the lap, tucking into a soup or casserole and watching *Shortland Street*.

The onion and carrot were some of the first vegetables I learnt to slice and dice when I began training as a chef. During my Japanese training, chef Takashi would put me through the paces, trying to get me to slice them as thin as wrapping paper. The knife wounds on my fingers made it look as if I'd been in the ring with kung fu legend Bruce Lee! I remember our delight at fooling diners into thinking they were eating noodles — we would place an onion in a vegetable lathe and create curly continuous 'noodles', plunging them in iced water to rid them of the their acid, then draining and dressing them with rice vinegar, sesame oil, shiso and mayonnaise.

I think of vegetables grown in the earth as comfort food: calming, not intimidating, affordable, gutsy rustic flavours, hidden away from the sun's harsh rays and a base for great recipes.

Socca

Makes 12

Smoked garlic

2 litres	water
1	carrot, peeled and chopped
2 stalks	celery, chopped
10cm	leek, washed and chopped
5	bay leaves
1 tablespoon	peppercorns
handful	fresh thyme
6	heads of garlic, pricked with a fork

In a deep saucepan, place the water, carrot, celery, leek, bay leaves, peppercorns and thyme. Bring to the boil.

Add the garlic and simmer for 40 minutes.

Drain and discard the poaching water.

Take a portable smoker that can fit onto your gas hobs or barbecue. Line the inside with tinfoil, scatter 2 cups manuka sawdust, turn the heat on and place the garlic on the trivet. When the smoker is smoking, place the lid on, turn down to a medium–low heat and smoke the garlic for approximately 30 minutes until golden in colour. Remove the garlic; it is ready to use.

This gluten-free flat bread is a specialty of Nice in France. I first discovered this at a dinner party given by Lyn Barnes, food editor of *NZ Life & Leisure* magazine. It had an interesting texture and I set about maximising its flavour by using four different onions and smothering it in smoked garlic oil whilst warm from the oven.

Socca

2 cups	chickpea flour (also called chana flour)
2 teaspoons	salt
2 teaspoons	freshly milled black pepper
2 cups	lukewarm water
10 tablespoons	olive oil
1	each of white, red and brown onion, peeled and thinly sliced
4	spring onions, thinly sliced on a bias
2 tablespoons	fresh rosemary leaves, chopped
3	heads of smoked garlic, peeled
2 tablespoons	American mustard
2 cups	vegetable oil

In a mixing bowl, sift the chickpea flour, salt and pepper. Slowly whisk in the water, add the olive oil, onions and rosemary and mix. Cover and allow to sit for 6 hours.

Preheat the oven to its hottest temperature. Put six omelette-sized (11 cm) cast-iron frying pans or two sauté pans into the oven and heat till very hot.

Meanwhile, using a hand blender, add in the garlic, mustard and vegetable oil and blend until smooth.

Remove the pans from the oven; turn down the oven temperature to 185°C.

Add a little oil to each pan, spoon in the mixture and place back into the oven and cook until firm and the edges are set.

Brush the surface of the socca with the smoked garlic oil and place under the grill to brown.

Cut into wedges, drizzled with more smoked garlic oil, flaky sea salt and milled black pepper.

Lyndsay's potato fritters

Makes 24 fritters

Fritters

2	large onions, peeled and finely chopped
4	eggs, beaten
½ cup	plain flour
½ cup	fresh herbs, chopped
1 teaspoon	salt
¼ teaspoon	freshly milled pepper
6	large potatoes, peeled and grated
4	carrots, peeled and grated
1	courgette, grated
½ cup	olive oil-based margarine
4 tablespoons	olive oil

In a large mixing bowl, combine the onion, eggs and flour. Stir in the herbs, salt and pepper, potatoes, carrots, courgette and margarine. Mix together well.

On a barbecue solid-top grill or thick-bottomed pan, heat the olive oil. Place on spoonfuls of batter, cook until golden, flip over and cook until golden on the other side.

If you are feeding a lot of hungry people, you can seal the fritters on both sides, transfer to a baking tray and finish cooking in a preheated 190°C oven for 5–6 minutes.

Gremolata

½ cup	brazil nuts, sliced thinly
1	orange, zested
½	orange, juiced
3	garlic cloves, peeled and finely chopped
1 cup	flat-leaf parsley, chopped
¼ cup	extra-virgin olive oil
	freshly milled salt and pepper

In a mixing bowl, toss the brazil nuts, orange zest and juice, garlic and parsley. In a steady stream, stir in the olive oil and season with salt and pepper.

It seems every mother has a challenge sneaking vegetables into their children's diets. Lyndsay was one such mum who created these vegetable fritters to achieve just that; however, she then had the problem of the adults devouring them too. Over the years, it hasn't been unusual for her to be asked to a barbecue as long as she brings a large bowl of fritter batter and some Thai sweet chilli sauce. I love these sensational morsels — they make a terrific brunch dish with runny poached eggs and gremolata.

Crispy prawn, carrot, pinenut and sultana salad

Serves 6

Curry vinaigrette

3 tablespoons	olive oil
1 tablespoon	curry powder
3	garlic cloves, peeled and finely chopped
½	onion, peeled and finely diced
1	orange, zested
1¼ cups	white wine vinegar
½ teaspoon	Tabasco sauce
2 teaspoons	American mustard
1 teaspoon	sugar
1¼ cups	olive oil
	freshly milled salt and pepper

In a sauté pan, add the first measure of olive oil and toast the curry powder with the garlic and onion until fragrant with the back of a spoon.

In a mixing bowl, whisk the curry powder base, orange zest, white wine vinegar, Tabasco sauce, mustard and sugar together.

Whisk in the second measure of olive oil and season with salt and pepper.

Each decade sets a certain food trend – in the 1980s, the French gave us nouvelle cuisine, which got a bad rap for small, pretty portions at big prices, but it also inspired the lighter, brighter and more interesting food we use today. In the 1990s, warm salads starting appearing in Californian restaurants, and a worldwide trend began of adding warm items to cold items for the evening meal. This quick dish smacks of crisp, aromatic and zingy flavours, and takes the humble carrot to a higher plane.

Salad

½ cup	sultanas, soaked in black English breakfast tea till plump
7	carrots, peeled, julienned and blanched
5	courgettes, julienned and blanched
1	Jazz apple, julienned
½ cup	pinenuts, toasted
¼ cup	sunflower seeds, toasted
¼ cup	coriander, roughly chopped
1kg	prawns, peeled and thinly sliced
⅓ cup	fine polenta (also known as cornmeal)
	sea salt

Drain the sultanas.

In a mixing bowl, add the sultanas, carrots, courgettes, apple, pinenuts, sunflower seeds and coriander and toss together.

Coat the prawns in fine polenta flour.

Heat a sauté pan, add 4 tablespoons of olive oil and add in the prawns; sauté until golden brown and crisp. Remove and drain the prawns on paper towels, and season with salt.

Toss the prawns through the carrot salad and dress with curry vinaigrette.

Kumara, spinach, tomato and ricotta bake

Serves 6

7	kumara, peeled, chopped and roasted
3 tablespoons	liquid honey
1/3 cup	olive oil
600g	spinach leaves, washed
1 teaspoon	nutmeg, grated
1/4 cup	sunflower seeds, toasted
10	ripe tomatoes, chopped
5	garlic cloves, peeled and finely chopped
1	onion, peeled and finely chopped
1/4 cup	basil leaves
1kg	ricotta cheese
5	eggs, beaten
1 cup	parmesan, grated
	freshly milled salt and pepper

Grease a baking dish with soft butter. Preheat the oven to 170°C.

Mash the roasted kumara with honey and olive oil. Push this mixture into the baking dish and level.

Heat a sauté pan with olive oil, add in the spinach leaves and wilt with the nutmeg and sunflower seeds.

Lay the spinach down on top of the kumara layer. Scatter over the tomatoes, garlic, onion and basil. Mix the ricotta and eggs together, lay over the top of the tomatoes and finish with the parmesan. Season the surface with salt and pepper.

Place the baking dish on a tray and slide into the oven. Bake for 45 minutes.

Allow to cool for 30 minutes before cutting into squares.

Serve the kumara bake with freshly picked salad greens and mandarin vinaigrette (see page 60).

Can you be a true blue New Zealander without spending some time near a beach, river or lake each summer? I would spend part of my school holidays surfcasting with my grandfather at Matata in the Bay of Plenty, escaping the fish for a moment to go to Granddad's friend's bach for a piece of this fantastic sweet potato bake. Perhaps Granddad's friend had once travelled to the Mediterranean, as the ricotta baked on top is so reminiscent of Italy.

Sea creatures

In New Zealand we are so lucky to be an island nation surrounded by a pristine coastline. For many, dangling a rod into the ocean starts in the early school years, as children hope to land a snapper or kingfish, often destined for the Kiwi smoker, that can outdo Dad's or Granddad's. According to Maori folklore, if you have the right sort of smell, you will catch fish all day when others do not get a bite!

It has become challenging to secure regular quantities of fish due to our strong export market. Fifteen years ago we would have regularly included snapper, orange roughy, hapuka or John Dory on the menu. Today we have to consider creating new dishes with species that simply weren't considered back then such as bluenose, gurnard, blue cod, ling and kahawai.

I love cooking fish with the skin attached. I am surprised when this method of preparation startles people; as long as the skin is scaled and crisped, it makes great crackling. Soft fish mousse can also be trapped under the skin and the fish simply steamed. For years I thought I had heard all the best tips about scaling fish until recently when I stumbled upon a fisherman who had just caught a hapuka (sea bass). With an animated audience watching from 5 metres away, the fisherman, armed with a waterblaster, proceeded to scale the fish with determination! If you don't have a water blaster at the ready, simply use a butter curler, a wide metal speed peeler or the back of a filleting knife to scrape off the scales then pat dry.

Chinese fish packages

Makes 12 parcels

1kg	tarakihi fillets (sea perch)
8	easy-peel mandarins, sliced thinly
1 stem	lemongrass, smashed and chopped
6	spring onions, sliced thinly on an angle
1 knob	fresh ginger, peeled and grated
6	garlic cloves, peeled and sliced
1	red onion, peeled and sliced thinly
12	easy-peel mandarins, juiced
12 teaspoons	sesame oil

Grease 12 rectangular sheets of tinfoil liberally.

Place on the tinfoil some of the mandarins, lemongrass, spring onion, ginger, garlic and red onion (these are called the aromatics). Slice the tarakihi into 3 pieces and arrange these on top of the aromatics. Top with more of the aromatics. Squeeze over some mandarin juice and 1 teaspoon of sesame oil over each parcel of fish. Bring the foil together over the fish to seal the package closed.

Place onto the barbecue and cook over a medium-low heat for approx 3–4 minutes. Remove from the barbecue and allow to cool slightly in the foil before eating.

Life as a first-time restaurateur in a town with abrupt high and low seasons creates challenges to one's bachelor lifestyle and the time off one can have. My little cottage nestled in macrocarpa trees is not complete without my well-used trusty barbecue. I was cooking a meal for a hot date, so I purchased some fresh fish, sprinkled over some Chinese flavours, raided my mandarin tree for an extra boost, wrapped it all in foil, turned off the barbecue and placed the fish under the hood. After the parcel was consumed, I awaited feedback — absolutely delicious, whew!

Sashimi of hapuka, Japanese guacamole and ponzu

Serves 6

Ponzu dressing

½ cup	sugar
1½ cups	Japanese rice vinegar
1¼ cups	low-salt Japanese soy sauce
2	lemons, zested and juiced
2	oranges, peeled and juiced
2	limes, peeled and juiced
2 tablespoons	kombu seaweed (can be substituted with three sushi nori sheets)
1 tablespoon	bonito flakes (can be substituted with piece of smoked kahawai fish)

Bring the sugar and rice vinegar to the boil, stirring to dissolve the sugar. Remove from the heat, stir in the remaining ingredients to infuse and leave to cool.

Refrigerate for one week, then strain and refrigerate until required.

Japanese guacamole

1	avocado, peeled and chopped
1 teaspoon	wasabi paste
½	large lime, juiced
1 teaspoon	sea salt

Toss the avocado into a food processor and blitz. Add in the wasabi, lime juice and salt; blitz until smooth and creamy.

Using a spatula, push the mixture through a sieve and refrigerate until needed.

1kg	hapuka fillets, no skin attached and each split into two lengthways
¼	white cabbage, shredded finely and soaked in iced water
2	Shanghai bok choy, washed and shredded finely
2 tablespoons	pickled ginger, julienned
10	mint leaves, julienned
¼ cup	white sesame seeds, toasted in a sauté pan

Assembly

Place a mound of guacamole on the plate and spread to 80mm in diameter.

Drain the cabbage, spinning it in a salad spinner to get rid of excess water.

In a mixing bowl, place the cabbage, bok choy, pickled ginger, mint leaves and sesame seeds. Mix together with a little of the ponzu.

Place a spoonful of cabbage on top of the guacamole.

With a sharp knife, slice the hapuka into thin slices and place over the cabbage, overlapping each piece.

Spoon some of the ponzu over the fish and serve immediately.

My early days of cooking took place in Wellington's first Japanese restaurant, Akiyoshi in Willis Street. I underwent the Karate Kid style of training: learning to cook with long chopsticks, polishing chefs' shoes and lessons on making wonderful green tea. It was strict training, which in later years has helped me to remain focused, driven and to achieve through the hardest times. This dish truly embraces the pure, uncomplicated, clean and fresh nature of Japanese food.

Crayfish crunch salad

Serves 6

Crayfish sauce

1kg	leftover crayfish shells
15 tablespoons	palm sugar or raw sugar
100ml	crayfish stock
125ml	tomato juice
125ml	lime juice
150ml	low-salt Japanese soy sauce
1 tablespoon	sesame oil
600ml	olive oil

To make the crayfish sauce, take the leftover shells, smash up and place into a saucepan with just enough cold water to cover them.

Bring to the boil, and simmer for 20 minutes.

Strain through a fine conical sieve, place back into a clean saucepan and reduce by half then strain again. Freeze this stock in an ice-cube tray; when frozen, pop out and place the cubes into snaplock bags.

In a saucepan, place in the sugar followed by the stock and take to a light caramel. Immediately whisk in the tomato juice, lime juice and soy, remove from the heat and allow to cool.

Whisk in the sesame and olive oils, and adjust the taste with sea salt flakes.

Recipes are often created spontaneously. I was once a chef for a high-profile wedding. The day after the wedding, a gourmet barbecue lunch was planned at a stunning location on the east coast of Kerikeri. The hungover guests stumbled off the bus followed by a diver who kindly plonked 40 crayfish at my feet, suggesting I might like to whip up a real treat! With the barbecue roaring, I watched the guests come back to life with the aromatic grilling of crayfish. The legend of the crayfish crunch salad was born.

Crunch salad

100ml	vegetable oil
10	garlic cloves, peeled and sliced thinly
2	red onions, peeled and sliced thinly
2	crayfish, cut in half lengthways
1	swede, peeled, julienned and soaked in cold water for 2 hours
1	green pawpaw or mango, peeled and julienned
¼ cup	thread coconut, lightly toasted
2	green chillies, seeded and julienned
4	easy-peel mandarins, peeled and segmented
5 tablespoons	raw peanuts, toasted and smashed in a tea towel
20	mint leaves, torn
¼ cup	coriander leaves
4	Kaffir lime leaves, julienned (optional)
6 tablespoons	jasmine rice dust

Get the barbecue solid-top grill very hot and pour on half the vegetable oil.

In two batches, add the garlic and red onion and cook until golden, draining on a kitchen towel. When both batches are cooked, place into a large mixing bowl.

Brush some the crayfish sauce over the exposed meat and place meat-side down on the grill.

Once the meat is cooked, brush over more of the sauce and allow to cool in the shell.

Remove the meat from the shell and cut into small pieces.

Place the drained swede into the mixing bowl. Use a salad spinner to remove any excess water which would thin down the sauce in the salad. Add to the mixing bowl the crayfish, green pawpaw, coconut and chillies and toss together. Lastly put in the mandarins, peanuts, mint, coriander and Kaffir lime leaves and toss together.

Drizzle over the warm sauce and toss together.

Place onto a large platter and sprinkle over roasted rice dust. This is easily achieved by toasting jasmine rice in a frying pan until it smells fragrant and then using a spice grinder to form a powder.

Poached oysters, ricotta gnocchi and prawn vinaigrette

Serves 6

When I was working at the exclusive Huka Lodge in Taupo, our sous chef Steve Harris had trained with Antony Worrall Thompson in England. He knocked me off my feet with this wonderful sweet, aromatic vinaigrette made from prawn meat and dessert wine. This adapted recipe warmed and basted over a nice chunk of bluenose is simply sublime. The vinaigrette will keep in the refrigerator for 3 weeks and is sensational with steamed Chinese chive flowers. If you have some Waiheke Island rock oysters, fill the shells with this vinaigrette, drop in the oysters and grill. It's a unique way of poaching the oysters and maximising the flavour.

Prawn vinaigrette

500g	raw prawn meat (Wairakei prawns from the geothermal farm are superb)
⅓ cup	cider vinegar
¼ cup	white wine
¼ cup	dessert wine
¼ cup	brandy
2 cups	olive oil
5	tomatoes, very ripe
½ cup	red onions, peeled and sliced thinly
½ cup	white of leeks, washed and chopped
½ cup	carrots, peeled and chopped
1 knob	fresh ginger, chopped
3	garlic cloves, peeled and chopped
1 tablespoon	coriander seeds
4 sprigs	thyme

Mix all the ingredients in a large saucepan thoroughly. Stir to the boil, and simmer slowly for 45 minutes without stirring.

Pass this vinaigrette through a conical strainer, pressing down on the solids to push out all the liquid. Discard the solids.

Gently reheat, and adjust the flavour with sea salt and milled pepper.

Continued overleaf

Ricotta gnocchi

1 cup	coarse fresh breadcrumbs (sourdough is great)
⅓ cup	extra virgin olive oil
3	garlic cloves, peeled and finely chopped
2 cups	ricotta cheese
⅓ cup	ground almonds
½ cup	plain flour
1 teaspoon	ground cinnamon, toasted in a pan
⅓ cup	parmesan, grated
3	eggs, lightly beaten

Preheat oven to 185°C.

In a bowl, combine the breadcrumbs, olive oil and garlic.

Line an oven tray with nonstick paper, scatter over the mixture and bake until golden, stirring occasionally. This takes approx 10–12 minutes. Cool and keep in an airtight container until needed.

Place ricotta in a large bowl and stir until smooth. Add in the almonds, flour, cinnamon, parmesan and eggs, mix until just combined.

Bring a saucepan of water to the boil.

Line a baking tray with nonstick paper and rub one palm of your hand with some olive oil. Place a little of the ricotta mixture in the oiled palm, then, using a tablespoon, scoop it from your hand and place into the water. You will need 24 gnocchi.

Once the gnocchi rises to the surface, scoop out with a slotted spoon and place onto the tray to cool.

36	Pacific rock oysters, shell and meat washed in cold salt water
6	tomatoes, deseeded and diced
½	cucumber, peeled, deseeded and diced
¼ cup	freshly picked mixed herbs such as tarragon, chervil, borage flowers and flat-leaf parsley
18	chive flowers, lightly steamed (optional)

Assembly

Preheat the grill.

Coat the oysters with the vinaigrette, place under the grill and just cook them through.

Place the gnocchi onto a warm plate and place the oysters in their shells in and around the gnocchi. Scatter over the tomato, cucumber and lastly the herbs. Spoon over a little more warmed prawn vinaigrette and finish with a scattering of garlic breadcrumbs.

Salmon

In my view, aquafarming is very much the way of the future. As our seas continue to be overfished, marine farms will become a common part of our life. The New Zealand salmon-farming industry is already well developed with its precision-run farms based in the pure waters of the Marlborough Sounds, Akaroa Harbour, the Rakaia River and Big Glory Bay, Stewart Island to name a few.

I remember my days learning to fillet fresh salmon, the blue silver-like skin glistening and the beautiful orange flesh. At the start I was petrified of hacking into the salmon, being sworn at by the chef and having to pay for a replacement fish with my apprentice's wages. What was even harder was trying to remove the pin bones with eyebrow tweezers or a plastic vegetable peeler. In utter frustration, I eventually borrowed my father's needle-nose pliers from his workshop and have used them ever since.

Kiwis just love salmon however you give it to them: eggs benedict with salmon; on bagels with cream cheese, lemon and capers; tossed through warm fettuccine pasta — the list goes on.

We are able to purchase fresh salmon, pin boned, ready to cook and at a competitive price. A fantastic and versatile fish high in Omega-3, it deserves to have its own chapter in this book.

Smoked salmon hash browns

Serves 6

4	potatoes, peeled and cut in half
2	eggs, beaten
1 tablespoon	sea salt
3 tablespoons	clarified butter
6	field mushrooms (portobello mushrooms)
4	garlic cloves, peeled and sliced
3 sprigs	rosemary, stripped
100ml	olive oil
¼ cup	white wine vinegar
6	eggs, free range preferred
18	smoked salmon slices
½ cup	aioli (French garlic mayonnaise)

There is no doubt that homemade potato hash browns with fresh herbs are far better than the frozen variety. I was concerned that the original recipe for hash browns made with raw grated potato would turn grey and unappealing if the potato was left out. I had read of Jewish people during the Hanukkah festival making latkes, a pre-cooked potato pancake that used grated potato fried in oil and could be frozen without discolouring. Combine this with fellow chef Chris Hagan's special way of poaching eggs and a stylish brunch dish was born.

Hash browns

In a saucepan place in the potatoes and cover with cold water. Bring to the boil, reduce heat and simmer for 4 minutes, drain and place potatoes on a tray to cool.

Once cool, finely grate the potatoes. In a bowl, bind the potatoes with the egg and salt.

With hands dipped in water, mould the potato mixture into 5cm-diameter patties.

Heat the clarified butter in a frying pan, add patties and fry on both sides until golden and cooked through.

Meanwhile, heat the oven to 180°C. Line a tray with foil and drizzle over a little olive oil. Place the mushrooms on the tray, scatter over the garlic, rosemary, sea salt and milled pepper. Pour over the olive oil and bake for 12 minutes or until cooked through.

Chris's poached eggs

In a saucepan, bring a litre of water to the boil with 1 tablespoon of salt.

Take a tea cup, add in a little white wine vinegar and crack an egg into it.

Stir the water in one direction, pop in the egg, and turn down to a simmer, poaching for 2–3 minutes so the egg white is cooked but the yolk is still runny.

To assemble, place a hash brown on the plate, add a portobello mushroom, a poached egg, 3 slices of smoked salmon and a dollop of aioli.

Scandinavian cured salmon

For one side of salmon

1 cup	demerara sugar
1	orange, zested and juiced
1	grapefruit, zested and juiced
½ cup	volcanic salt (iodised salt can be used)
1 tablespoon	mixed peppercorns (pink, green and black)
½ cup	dill, fronds picked
1 knob	fresh ginger, peeled and grated
1	side of salmon, pin boned, skin attached and cut in half

Combine all ingredients except salmon and grind in a pestle and mortar.

Cut the salmon to the length of a snaplock bag. Place some of the mixture into the bag, add the salmon and cover with more mixture. Seal the bag shut, swish the mixture around and refrigerate overnight.

Remove the salmon from the bag, scrape off the excess salt. Slice the salmon thinly and serve with button mushrooms roasted with cinnamon butter, soft feta cheese and mandarin vinaigrette.

Mandarin vinaigrette

2 tablespoons	olive oil
¼ cup	shallots, peeled and finely diced
8	easy-peel mandarins, juiced
1	orange, zested
2 tablespoons	caster sugar
1 tablespoon	Dijon mustard
2 cups	olive oil

In a saucepan over medium heat, heat the olive oil and shallots; cook until shallots are transparent and tender. Add the mandarin juice, orange zest and sugar and reduce the liquid by half.

Pour the mixture into a bowl, whisk in the mustard and then the olive oil. Taste, adjust the flavour with salt and the consistency with hot water if needed.

While I was working in New York in 2000, I had the chance to sneak away for lunch at Aquavit, where I was inspired by Marcus Samuelsson's modern interpretation of Scandanavian cuisine. I reflected about how popular gravlax is in New Zealand and on the 16-hour flight home I developed a contemporary version of this classic. Volcanic salt, with its natural minerals, makes a big difference to the curing process and is becoming more readily available. With the zing of grapefruit juice and the aromatic dill fronds, the flavour and moisture of the salmon are truly stunning. I personally find it easier to use a parmesan grater for grating the ginger and a microplane for zesting the fruit.

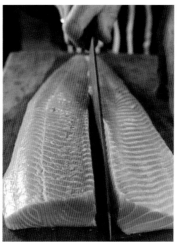

Sake-pickled salmon, rice and cucumber

Serves 6

Sake pickle

1 tablespoon	coriander seeds
½ tablespoon	white peppercorns
1 tablespoon	mustard seeds
1	cinnamon stick
2	bay leaves
1 tablespoon	Gregg's chilli lime seasoning
2	star anise (optional)
1	red onion, peeled and sliced thinly
2 tablespoons	crushed ginger
1 cup	sake rice wine
2 cups	Japanese rice vinegar
½ cup	sugar
1 tablespoon	salt

600g	salmon fillet, pin boned and cut into 20mm cubes
1	cucumber, peeled, cut in half and deseeded
1	avocado, peeled, cut in half and sliced
4 tablespoons	white sesame seeds, toasted
3 cups	cooked brown rice

In a saucepan, bring all the sake pickle ingredients to a boil, reduce heat and simmer for 4 minutes.

Meanwhile, place the salmon and cucumber in a bowl. Strain the sake pickle straight over the salmon and cucumber, cover with cling film for 10 minutes. Uncover, remove the salmon and cucumber.

Strain the pickling juice, reserving 50ml (the remaining juice can be refrigerated and used again).

In a serving bowl, place the brown rice, top with the salmon cubes, cucumber, avocado, sesame seeds and reserved pickling juice.

Each year I present an entertaining, high-energy cooking show at the Ellerslie International Flower Show. One of the demonstrations is the supermarket 'bang for your buck' segment where each chef buys ten dollars worth of groceries for another chef to prepare, often choosing items the other chef loathes eating. When I reviewed my colleague's choice I found he had included a can of baked beans; maybe every other Kiwi's favourite but not mine! The food gods were smiling on me that day as I discovered some chilli lime seasoning in our Gregg's pantry of ingredients. My dish was given a lifeline. And the can of baked beans? It was tossed into the audience with great pleasure.

Lasagna of salmon, mushroom and rocket

Serves 8

Lemon béchamel

¼ cup	butter, diced
25g	Mighty Mushrooms oyster mushroom powder
1	lemon, zested
¼ cup	flour
1 litre	nonfat milk, warmed

Melt the butter in a saucepan over medium heat and stir in the mushroom powder and lemon zest. Add in the flour, turn down the heat to low and cook out the flour for 4 minutes. Stirring constantly, add small amounts of milk until amalgamated. Bring the sauce to a gentle simmer, season with salt and milled pepper and remove from the heat.

The way a dish is described on a menu can often be the reason why it does or doesn't sell. Everybody knows what lasagna is — however, if I added porcini, some diners would think I'd created something scary and inedible! I needed my salmon lasagna to have some earthy flavours and came across a dried mushroom powder produced in Waimate North by Mighty Mushrooms. Combined with some lemon, rocket leaves and a little of my parmesan oil, it delivers a sensational lasagna with the wow factor.

Lasagna

¼ cup	olive oil
400g	button mushrooms, sliced
½ cup	sour cream
8	fresh pasta sheets, cooked
200g	salmon, sliced
1 cup	rocket leaves (arugula)
3 tablespoons	parsley, chopped
150g	parmesan, grated

Preheat the oven to 175°C.

In a sauté pan, heat the olive oil, add in the mushrooms and sauté until soft. Add in the sour cream and mix together.

Take a roasting pan and grease the sides and bottom of the pan with a little oil. Lay 2 sheets of pasta in the bottom of the pan, overlapping each other. Spoon over a little of the sauce, lay down about one fifth of the salmon and rocket leaves.

Lay down 2 more overlapping sheets of pasta. Spoon over the mushroom mixture, parsley and two-thirds of the parmesan.

Make another layer with 2 overlapping sheets of pasta. Spoon over a little more of the sauce, salmon and rocket leaves.

Lay down the final 2 sheets of overlapping pasta, drizzle over olive oil and scatter with the remaining one-third of parmesan.

Cover the lasagna with greased baking paper and seal with a piece of foil. Bake for 20–30 minutes until cooked through. Allow to cool before cutting.

Tomatoes

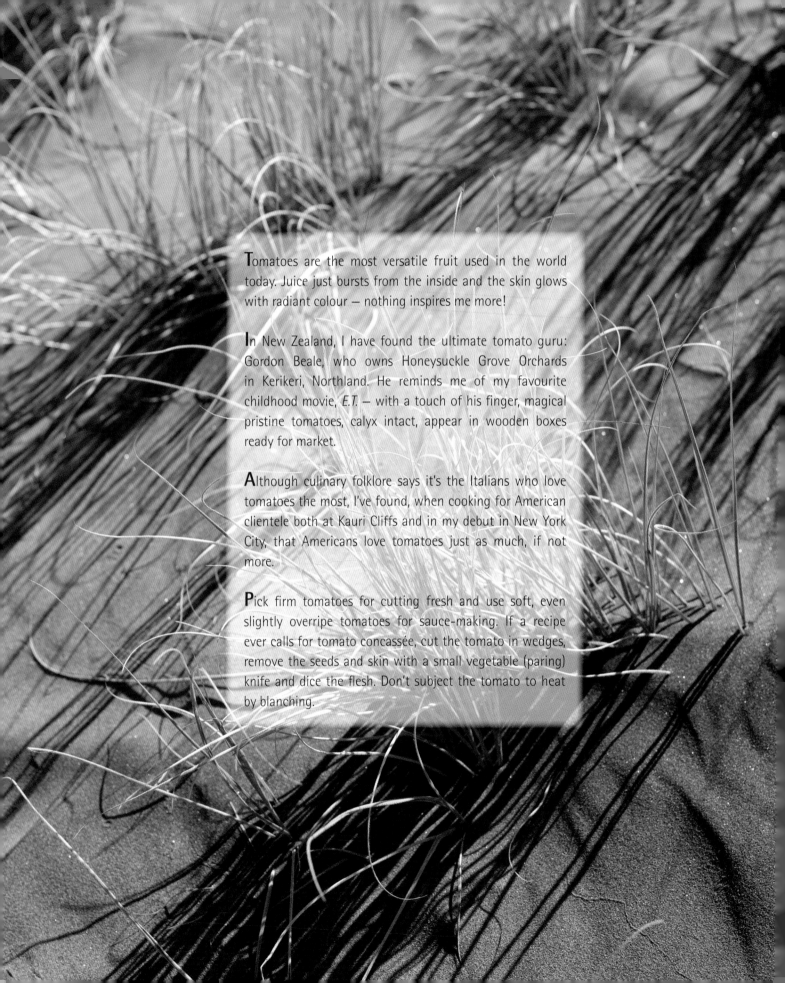

Tomatoes are the most versatile fruit used in the world today. Juice just bursts from the inside and the skin glows with radiant colour — nothing inspires me more!

In New Zealand, I have found the ultimate tomato guru: Gordon Beale, who owns Honeysuckle Grove Orchards in Kerikeri, Northland. He reminds me of my favourite childhood movie, *E.T.* — with a touch of his finger, magical pristine tomatoes, calyx intact, appear in wooden boxes ready for market.

Although culinary folklore says it's the Italians who love tomatoes the most, I've found, when cooking for American clientele both at Kauri Cliffs and in my debut in New York City, that Americans love tomatoes just as much, if not more.

Pick firm tomatoes for cutting fresh and use soft, even slightly overripe tomatoes for sauce-making. If a recipe ever calls for tomato concassée, cut the tomato in wedges, remove the seeds and skin with a small vegetable (paring) knife and dice the flesh. Don't subject the tomato to heat by blanching.

Tomato sorbet and melon gazpacho

Serves 4

Tomato sorbet

¼ cup	tomato juice
¼ cup	sugar
¼ cup	liquid glucose (corn syrup)
750g	canned chopped tomatoes
½	orange, zested
4	basil leaves, sliced
1 teaspoon	salt
pinch	cayenne pepper
1 tablespoon	red wine vinegar
1 tablespoon	parmesan-infused olive oil

In a saucepan, place the tomato juice, sugar and glucose and heat until a clear syrup is formed (about 3–5 minutes). Pour in the canned tomatoes and orange zest, and simmer for a further 5 minutes. Add in the basil, salt, cayenne pepper, red wine vinegar and parmesan oil, stirring to combine together.

Place the mixture into an ice-cream maker to churn and freeze overnight. Alternatively, pour it onto flat trays with a lip, freeze then process in a food processor, refreeze and serve as a granita.

Melon gazpacho

⅓ cup	manuka honey
1	rock melon, peeled, seeded and diced
½	lemon, juiced
4	mint leaves
100g	cucumber, peeled, seeded and diced
50g	celery, peeled and chopped
1 teaspoon	fresh ginger, peeled and grated
½ cup	extra-virgin olive oil
2 teaspoons	sea salt

In a saucepan, melt the honey and add in the rock melon. Stir together till the melon starts to soften then transfer to a blender. Add the remaining ingredients and blend until smooth. Pass through a fine sieve and adjust the taste with more salt if required.

This is one of my all-time favourite recipes. It just sings of long, hot summer days, relaxing by the pool and alfresco dining. Classic chilled gazpacho soup originates in Spain and includes Spanish sherry vinegar, stale breadcrumbs and delicious extra-virgin olive oil. The tomato sorbet above gives the soup a sophisticated and mysterious element, and is fantastic with some of my parmesan-infused olive oil from First Drop olive growers.

Tomato tarte tatin

Serves 4

Onion jam

50g	clarified butter
2	onions, peeled and sliced thinly
4 sprigs	thyme leaves (pizza thyme leaves are the best)
2 tablespoons	brown sugar

Heat a nonstick sauté pan, add the butter, onions, thyme and sugar, and cook together on a high heat for 3 minutes.

Turn the heat down to low, add in a little water, cover with a lid and continue to cook for 10 minutes until the onions are soft and caramelised.

Blitz in a food processor to create a jam-like texture and place in a bowl until required.

Tomato lemon vinaigrette

½	preserved lemon, rind only and diced
1	chilli, deseeded and finely diced
4	tomatoes, deseeded and diced
1 teaspoon	American mustard
1 teaspoon	thyme leaves
¼ cup	white wine vinegar
150ml	extra-virgin olive oil
	salt and freshly milled pepper

In a mixing bowl, place all the ingredients except the olive oil and mix together.

Stir in the olive oil in a steady stream. Adjust the taste with sea salt and pepper, and the texture with a little warm water.

Tarte Tatin was first created by accident at the Hôtel Tatin in France in 1889. The hotel was run by two sisters, Stéphanie and Caroline Tatin. Legend has it that one day, Stéphanie, overworked, started to make a traditional apple pie but left the apples cooking for too long. She tried to rescue the dish by putting the pastry base on top of the pan of apples, and quickly finished the cooking by putting the whole pan in the oven. She then served the upside-down tart to her hotel guests for dessert, and was surprised to find how much they enjoyed it. History was made . . .

Tarte tatin

2 sheets	ready rolled puff pastry
1	egg, beaten with 1 tablespoon milk
7	tomatoes, sliced
1 cup	feta cheese, cubed or crumbled
¼ cup	pinenuts, toasted in balsamic vinegar
handful	rocket (arugula) leaves

Preheat the oven to 200°C.

Cut the puff pastry into 4x10cm diameter discs and place onto nonstick baking paper. Prick the pastry with a fork, brush with egg wash, scatter over sea salt flakes and bake in the oven for 5 minutes until light golden in colour. Turn the discs over and bake for a further 5 minutes. Remove from the oven.

Turn oven temperature down to 185°C.

Line a blini pan or tart tin with a circle of nonstick baking paper. Drizzle the paper with a little olive oil, then place the sliced tomato, starting with a disc in the centre, then overlapping around the pan.

Spread a spoonful of onion jam over the tomato layer and secure the pastry disc on top by pushing the sides of the pastry down around the edge of the tomatoes.

Place into the oven to finish cooking until the pastry is dark golden all over (about 10 minutes).

Invert onto a plate so the tomatoes are on top.

Scatter over some feta and pinenuts, some of the vinaigrette and a cluster of rocket leaves and serve.

Emma's spaghetti Bolognese

Serves 6

2 tablespoons	extra-virgin olive oil
1	onion, peeled, diced and processed
4	garlic cloves, peeled and finely chopped
4 stalks	celery, finely diced
2	carrots, finely grated
4 rashers	bacon, diced
2 cups	beef mince
2 cups	pork mince
¾ cup	tomato purée
1 cup	whole milk
1 cup	red wine
1 cup	water
4 sprigs	thyme leaves
1 teaspoon	salt
½ teaspoon	black pepper
300g	dried spaghetti pasta
50g	butter, diced
2 tablespoons	parmesan-infused olive oil

Preheat an electric frying pan to its highest temperature.

Add the olive oil, then the onion, garlic, celery and carrot, stirring occasionally until softened (about 5 minutes, with the lid on). Add the bacon and the beef and pork mince and stir, breaking up lumps, until no longer pink (about 10 minutes, without the lid). Stir in tomato purée, milk, wine, water and thyme, cover and simmer until sauce is thickened (about 45 minutes). Add salt and pepper and remove from heat.

Meanwhile, bring a saucepan of salted water to the boil. Add the pasta and cook until it is just firm to the bite in the centre (al dente). Drain the pasta through a colander, reserving 150ml of the pasta water.

In the same saucepan, heat the reserved pasta water and whisk in the butter and parmesan oil until it has blended to make an emulsion. Mix this coating through the spaghetti.

Mix the mince sauce through the spaghetti.

Serve with freshly grated parmesan or pecorino cheese and freshly milled pepper.

This dish is top of the pops with university students throughout New Zealand. It was a real eye-opener to watch my partner's daughter whip up a teenage shortcut version of the Italian classic from Bologna, executed in my nana's warped Zip electric frying pan! This is a consistent dish for kids to perfect before leaving home.

Roast tomato and pistachio knapsacks

Serves 8

1kg	tomatoes, cut in half
8	garlic cloves, roasted in their skins and peeled
40g	tomato paste in the tube
2	red chillies, blackened in the skin and peeled
¼ cup	pistachio kernels, smashed in a tea towel
8	basil leaves, diced
	salt and pepper
1	lemon, zested
150g	butter, diced and melted
1	sheet of filo pastry

This recipe was created out of sheer desperation. As head chef of a very busy restaurant in Darlinghurst, Sydney, I arrived at work one day to find wooden crutches leaning up against the large front window along with angry slogans in chalk from a supplier for not paying the bills! I had our regulars, the *Flying Doctors* television crew, in that evening and this is all I had on hand to create a nightly special. They loved it; it became a signature dish and reminded me that pastry items always sell.

Preheat the oven to 220°C.

Grease a deep oven dish, drizzle over some olive oil and toss in the tomatoes. Place into the top part of the oven and roast until they start to colour and break down (about 45 minutes).

Drain the tomatoes in a sieve, preferably overnight. Freeze the leftover tomato jus for a fine tomato jelly or vinaigrette.

Place the tomatoes in a bowl, add in the tomato paste, red chillies, pistachios and basil and stir together. Season with sea salt and milled pepper to taste.

Mix the lemon zest through the melted butter.

Reduce oven temperature to 180°C.

On a floured chopping board, lay out a sheet of filo pastry and brush it with the lemon butter. Place another sheet on top, brush with more lemon butter and finish with a top sheet, smoothing it out with your hand.

Cut the filo stack into eight equal squares, and place a spoonful of filling in the middle of each square. Gather the filo up around the filling and secure at the top, so it resembles the top of a knapsack. Place the filo parcels onto a greased baking sheet.

Bake until golden (about 5–6 minutes) and serve.

These taste fantastic served with a courgette fritter and basil pesto blended with roasted red pepper.

Beef and lamb

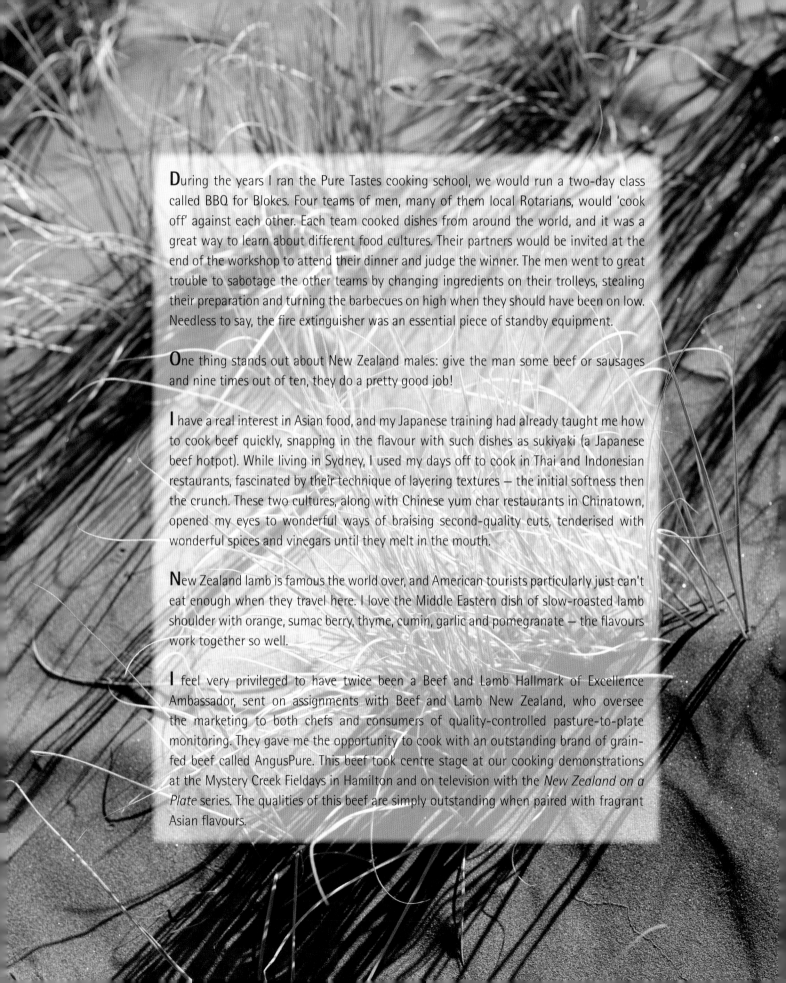

During the years I ran the Pure Tastes cooking school, we would run a two-day class called BBQ for Blokes. Four teams of men, many of them local Rotarians, would 'cook off' against each other. Each team cooked dishes from around the world, and it was a great way to learn about different food cultures. Their partners would be invited at the end of the workshop to attend their dinner and judge the winner. The men went to great trouble to sabotage the other teams by changing ingredients on their trolleys, stealing their preparation and turning the barbecues on high when they should have been on low. Needless to say, the fire extinguisher was an essential piece of standby equipment.

One thing stands out about New Zealand males: give the man some beef or sausages and nine times out of ten, they do a pretty good job!

I have a real interest in Asian food, and my Japanese training had already taught me how to cook beef quickly, snapping in the flavour with such dishes as sukiyaki (a Japanese beef hotpot). While living in Sydney, I used my days off to cook in Thai and Indonesian restaurants, fascinated by their technique of layering textures — the initial softness then the crunch. These two cultures, along with Chinese yum char restaurants in Chinatown, opened my eyes to wonderful ways of braising second-quality cuts, tenderised with wonderful spices and vinegars until they melt in the mouth.

New Zealand lamb is famous the world over, and American tourists particularly just can't eat enough when they travel here. I love the Middle Eastern dish of slow-roasted lamb shoulder with orange, sumac berry, thyme, cumin, garlic and pomegranate — the flavours work together so well.

I feel very privileged to have twice been a Beef and Lamb Hallmark of Excellence Ambassador, sent on assignments with Beef and Lamb New Zealand, who oversee the marketing to both chefs and consumers of quality-controlled pasture-to-plate monitoring. They gave me the opportunity to cook with an outstanding brand of grain-fed beef called AngusPure. This beef took centre stage at our cooking demonstrations at the Mystery Creek Fieldays in Hamilton and on television with the *New Zealand on a Plate* series. The qualities of this beef are simply outstanding when paired with fragrant Asian flavours.

Sirloin steak, onion rings and mash

Serves 8

White bean aioli

500g	lima beans, soaked overnight in cold water, drained and rinsed
300g	agria or Maori potatoes, peeled, cut in half and steamed
4	garlic cloves, peeled and finely chopped
325ml	natural unsweetened yoghurt
125ml	extra-virgin olive oil

In a saucepan, place the lima beans and cover with plenty of cold water, bring to the boil and simmer until cooked (about 45 minutes). Allow the beans to cool down in the water. (If you were to drain them straightaway, they would dehydrate and split open.)

In a food processor, place the drained lima beans and blend until smooth. Add in the potato, garlic and yoghurt, blend until smooth. With the motor running, pour in the olive oil.

Taste and adjust the flavour with salt and milled pepper.

Baked field mushrooms

5 tablespoons	olive oil
	sea salt and pepper
8	large field (portobello) mushrooms
8	garlic cloves, peeled and sliced thinly
3 sprigs	rosemary, leaves stripped and stem discarded
200ml	parmesan-infused olive oil

Preheat the oven to 175°C.

Line a baking sheet with tinfoil and drizzle over the olive oil. Season the tinfoil with sea salt and freshly milled pepper. Arrange the mushrooms on the tray and sprinkle over the garlic and rosemary. Drizzle over the parmesan oil and bake in the oven for 7 minutes, then turn the mushrooms over and bake for a further 7 minutes.

Remove from the oven and store in an airtight container in the refrigerator till needed.

Cooking for a bunch of rugby players is pretty straightforward: don't intimidate them and give them something they know. This dish sounded marvellous when I ran it past the lads — little did they know that the dish has a twist that would take their tastebuds to a new frontier. The onion rings are made with a gluten-free Indian bhaji batter, the field mushrooms roasted in my parmesan oil with rosemary and garlic, and the mash made from dried white lima beans, potato and plain yoghurt. The dish was declared delicious and when told what they had eaten, the verdict was 'That's very unusual!' Needless to say, they have become New Zealand's gourmet rugby team.

Onion bhaji

2	onions, peeled and cut into thin rings
½ teaspoon	salt
300g	gram or chickpea flour
½ teaspoon	chilli powder
1 teaspoon	turmeric powder
1 tablespoon	cumin seeds
½ teaspoon	ajowan seeds, or brown mustard seeds
¾ cup	L&P soft drink

Sprinkle the onions with salt, cover with just enough water and put them aside for 15 minutes.

Heat a deep-fryer or wok to 180°C. (You might need to check the temperature with a cooking thermometer if you are using a wok.)

In a mixing bowl, place flour, chilli, turmeric, cumin and ajowan seeds and mix with enough L&P to make a fairly thick batter.

Drain the onion rings and stir into the batter. Drop the rings into the hot oil and deep-fry until golden. Drain on absorbent paper.

Assembly

8 x 220g	sirloin or porterhouse steaks
50ml	raspberry vinegar
3 tablespoons	table salt
	vegetable oil
handful	watercress tips

Heat the barbecue grill until very hot.

Rub the steaks all over with the raspberry vinegar and then season with salt.

Brush the vegetable oil over the grill. Cook the steaks to your liking, turning them over halfway through the grilling process. Once done, allow to rest off the heat for 4 minutes before serving.

Meanwhile, warm the field mushrooms on the grill.

Place a mound of white bean aioli in the centre of a plate and spread slightly with the back of a spoon. Place the steak on top of the aioli, and top with a mushroom, some onion bhaji and sprigs of watercress.

Spanish lamb chops, watermelon and feta

Romesco sauce

2	red bell peppers, roasted and skin removed
6	garlic cloves, roasted in their skins until soft
2	tomatoes, cut into wedges
2	chillies, seeded and finely chopped
3 tablespoons	sherry vinegar
¾ cup	extra-virgin olive oil
1 cup	brazil nuts, toasted and crushed
	sea salt and milled pepper

In a food processor, place the peppers and the garlic popped out of its skin and blend quickly. Add the tomato, chillies and sherry vinegar and blitz to a paste. With the motor running, pour in the olive oil.

Remove from the food processor, scooping into a mixing bowl, and fold in the brazil nuts. Season this with sea salt and freshly milled pepper.

If this sauce is too thick, thin down with a little boiling water.

Lamb chop crust

3 teaspoons	ground cumin
1 teaspoon	caraway seeds
1 teaspoon	fenugreek seeds, ground
1 teaspoon	ground cardamom
1 teaspoon	fennel seeds, ground
1 teaspoon	mustard seeds, soaked in water overnight and drained
¼ cup	manchego cheese (a hard cheese made from sheep's milk. Substitute with parmesan if necessary)
100g	sourdough crumbs
¼ cup	olive oil

In a mixing bowl, mix all the spices together. Toss in the breadcrumbs and mix well. Bind together with the olive oil to make a crumble.

What's the latest food trend? Spanish food has made the culinary world stand up and take notice. Spaniard Ferran Adria has brought molecular gastronomy to the fore. Where else would you find natural fruit jellies made from frozen extra-virgin olive oil, ribbons of pasta made from sea kelp or layered hot and cold soup of tomato and basil, the basil aroma sprayed around by a waiter as you eat the tomato soup! I pay homage to Spain's regional food, which is full flavoured, rustic and exciting. My Chilean chef, Javier Robles, introduced me to this romesco sauce which cries out to be served with lamb and manchego cheese.

Lamb chop dish

Serves 4

8 large	midloin lamb chops
2 tablespoons	fresh thyme leaves
	parmesan oil
	sea salt and milled pepper
2 cups	watermelon, peeled and diced
2 cups	feta, cut into cubes
500g	fresh beans, blanched for 2 minutes

Preheat the oven to 185°C.

Heat a large sauté pan, add in some olive oil, season the lamb chops with sea salt and milled pepper and fry on both sides to seal the lamb.

Remove from the heat and top with the crust; bake in the oven for 6 minutes. Remove and rest for 4 minutes.

In a mixing bowl, toss the beans with the thyme and parmesan oil.

Place a spoonful of romesco sauce on the plate and spread lengthways with a spoon. Spoon some of the beans onto the plate, drop over some of the watermelon and feta. Place lamb chop on top and serve.

Leftover roast lamb pie

Serves 8 hungry people

Best short pastry ever

265g	butter, softened
375g	plain flour, sifted
1½ teaspoons	salt
1½ teaspoons	caster sugar
1 tablespoon	chilled water
1	egg, beaten
1 teaspoon	white vinegar

My Nana Mabel was a wee Englishwoman whose kitchen was her territory, my grandfather treading carefully whenever he entered. As a child I managed to con my way into her domain, admiring her approach to her dainty food. Nana was amazing when it came to using leftovers; wartime deprivations had taught her how to be efficient with ingredients. This roast lamb pie is an incredible example. She often tossed in little pieces of crisped black pudding or slices of lambs' kidneys roasted in bacon fat for a classic English flavour.

In a mixing bowl, cream the butter until soft. Add in the flour and salt, and rub until it resembles fine breadcrumbs. Add in the sugar and mix.

Beat the water, egg and white vinegar together and mix in until it forms a stiff dough.

Tip onto a bench and, with a little extra flour, knead till it is smooth and soft. Cut the dough into four pieces, wrap in cling film and refrigerate or freeze until needed.

Wipe the bench with a wet cloth, line the area with two overlapping pieces of cling film and dust with flour.

Place a piece of dough on the cling film and dust the dough with flour. Place another two pieces of cling film over the dough and, with a rolling pin, roll the dough out between the cling film into a circle one third larger than a 26cm nonstick springform tin.

Take the cling film off the top of the pastry, and invert the pastry into the tin, pressing down in the corners and overlapping the sides. With the cling film still inside the tin, fill with baking beans such as chickpeas or lentils and place the tin into the freezer for 30 minutes.

Meanwhile, preheat the oven to 165°C.

Bake the pastry for 15 minutes, remove the cling film and baking beans, and place back into the oven to cook the bottom of the pie base for 5 minutes. Take out of the oven and cool. Cut off the excess pastry at the top of the tin with a sharp knife.

Roast lamb pie

1	lamb shoulder, boned and rolled, or 1kg leftover pieces
3 tablespoons	vegetable oil
2 sprigs	rosemary, snapped into short pieces
6	garlic cloves, peeled and cut in half
2 tablespoons	manuka honey boiled with 2 tablespoons water
1 tablespoon	cracked black pepper
1	carrot, peeled and diced
2 sticks	celery, diced
½	leek, washed and diced
1	onion, peeled and diced
1 tablespoon	HP sauce
3 tablespoons	red wine
400ml	beef stock
	leftover pan juices from the roast
1 tablespoon	arrowroot, mixed with 2 tablespoons water
2 cups	leftover mashed potato
1 tablespoon	cream
½ cup	grated cheddar cheese

Preheat the oven to 195°C.

For those who don't have leftover lamb pieces to make this pie, start by making 12 inserts with a small knife through the netting of the lamb and rub the oil all over. Push a piece of rosemary and garlic into the inserts.

Spray a cooling rack with oil, place the rack into a deep-sided roasting pan, put the lamb on the rack, pour over the honey and scatter the pepper. Pour 1 cup of water into the roasting pan.

Place into the oven and roast for 20 minutes then turn the heat down to 160°C and continue to roast for 1 hour.

When the lamb has finished roasting, heat a saucepan with oil, add in the carrot, celery, leek and onion, stir for 3 minutes. Add in the HP sauce, red wine and beef stock, bring to a simmer and cook for 8 minutes. Add in the roasting juices with some of the rosemary and garlic that has popped out during cooking. Bring to the boil and simmer for a further 4 minutes then whisk in the arrowroot to thicken the sauce. Stir in the lamb pieces and pour into the pie base.

Spoon the leftover mashed potato over the top, making marks in the surface with the tines of a fork. Brush the surface with the cream and scatter over the cheese.

Bake in a preheated 170°C oven for 30 minutes.

Sweet Thai crispy beef and coconut rice

Serves 6

500g	lean beef such as rump or topside, shredded thinly
100ml	peanut oil
50ml	sesame oil
12	shallots, peeled and sliced thinly
6	garlic cloves, peeled and sliced thinly
½ cup	raw sugar
½ cup	mint leaves, chopped roughly
½ cup	coriander leaves, chopped roughly
150ml	fish sauce
7	limes, juiced

Deep-fry the shallots and garlic in not-too-hot oil until golden, draining on absorbent paper.

Place all of the ingredients into a bowl, mix together and infuse in the fridge for 2 hours.

Drain the liquor and reserve.

In a smoking-hot wok, fry the beef quickly in small batches, keeping it raw in the middle. Put back into the liquor.

Coconut rice

2 cups	jasmine rice, washed clear in a sieve
1½ cups	coconut cream
1½ cups	cold water
2	limes, rolled, cut and juiced

Place the washed rice into a thick-bottomed saucepan or rice cooker. Mix the coconut cream and water together and add to the rice.

Stir to the boil, and turn the heat down to the lowest possible heat and cover the saucepan with a lid. Simmer the rice for 15 minutes, then remove from the heat, leaving the lid on, and rest for another 15 minutes.

Remove the lid, fluff up the rice and stir in the lime juice.

Place a mound of warm coconut rice in the centre of the plate (we use a cookie cutter and press the rice into this).

Spoon the beef around and top with a favourite relish such as mango or cucumber and serve. For an extra touch, scatter over crushed peanuts or cashews, some coconut cream and crispy shallots.

This is a simple dish that has followed me around for the last 10 years. For a long time I tried desperately to keep this a secret but finally I was persuaded to film the dish in 2008 for *New Zealand on a Plate* for Sky Food television. This dish is great for the whole family; children in the restaurant often preferred this over the children's menu and I have often knocked it together for friends at their homes on my day off.

Nuts and spices

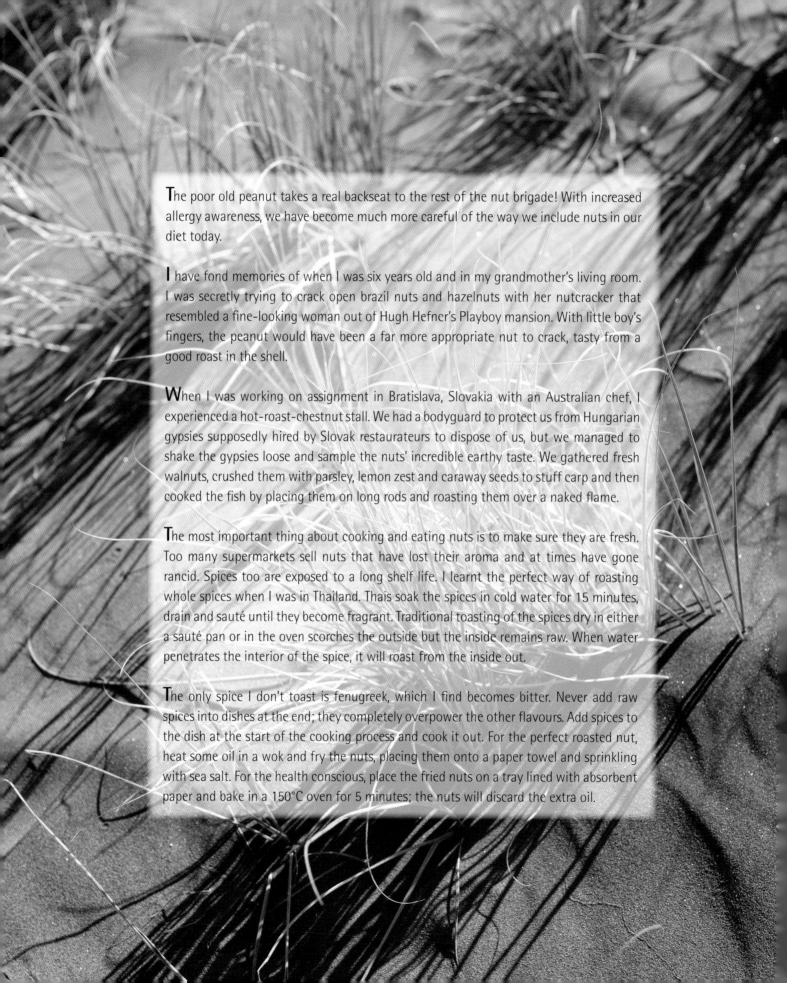

The poor old peanut takes a real backseat to the rest of the nut brigade! With increased allergy awareness, we have become much more careful of the way we include nuts in our diet today.

I have fond memories of when I was six years old and in my grandmother's living room. I was secretly trying to crack open brazil nuts and hazelnuts with her nutcracker that resembled a fine-looking woman out of Hugh Hefner's Playboy mansion. With little boy's fingers, the peanut would have been a far more appropriate nut to crack, tasty from a good roast in the shell.

When I was working on assignment in Bratislava, Slovakia with an Australian chef, I experienced a hot-roast-chestnut stall. We had a bodyguard to protect us from Hungarian gypsies supposedly hired by Slovak restaurateurs to dispose of us, but we managed to shake the gypsies loose and sample the nuts' incredible earthy taste. We gathered fresh walnuts, crushed them with parsley, lemon zest and caraway seeds to stuff carp and then cooked the fish by placing them on long rods and roasting them over a naked flame.

The most important thing about cooking and eating nuts is to make sure they are fresh. Too many supermarkets sell nuts that have lost their aroma and at times have gone rancid. Spices too are exposed to a long shelf life. I learnt the perfect way of roasting whole spices when I was in Thailand. Thais soak the spices in cold water for 15 minutes, drain and sauté until they become fragrant. Traditional toasting of the spices dry in either a sauté pan or in the oven scorches the outside but the inside remains raw. When water penetrates the interior of the spice, it will roast from the inside out.

The only spice I don't toast is fenugreek, which I find becomes bitter. Never add raw spices into dishes at the end; they completely overpower the other flavours. Add spices to the dish at the start of the cooking process and cook it out. For the perfect roasted nut, heat some oil in a wok and fry the nuts, placing them onto a paper towel and sprinkling with sea salt. For the health conscious, place the fried nuts on a tray lined with absorbent paper and bake in a 150°C oven for 5 minutes; the nuts will discard the extra oil.

Lemon and macadamia tart

Makes a 26cm tart

Tart shell

- 2 cups flour
- 400g butter, chopped
- 1 cup sour cream

In a food processor, add in the flour and butter. Pulse the mixture until the butter is about the size of a macadamia nut. Add in the sour cream and pulse the mixture until just combined.

Place the dough onto a floured surface and roll out to a disc shape slightly larger than the springform tin you will use.

When Y2K arrived, I was in limbo after leaving Paramount Restaurant in Auckland and before moving to Kauri Cliffs Lodge in the Far North. Brent and Carol Cameron asked if I would play second fiddle in their restaurant in Waiuku. With Brent being a Beef and Lamb Hallmark of Excellence Ambassador I jumped at the chance to help out. In the process Carol decided I was destined to work as a commis waiter in the dining room under her tuition. I'm sure I became their comedy act on many nights. I kept forgetting to serve spoons with the soup and tried to tell the diners to eat it Fijian style!

As their cook, I was amazed at how many of these tarts we produced, and as a waiter I got to see the diners devour them. I've added lemon to this recipe to cut the richness and chosen sour-cream pastry for the base. This legendary tart showcases macadamias in the best possible way and is a real winner. It is lovely dusted with icing sugar and served with balsamic strawberries (toss in a bowl with a little balsamic vinegar, brown sugar, some julienned mint) and a scoop of either Tatua thickened cream, mascarpone or Barker's lemon curd.

Place onto two sheets of overlapped cling film, cover and leave to rest in the fridge for 30 minutes.

Preheat the oven to 170°C.

Place the pastry into the springform tin, pushing down in the corners with the cling film. Pour in some baking beans such as dried pulses or rice onto the cling film and bake for 20 minutes.

Remove the baking beans and cling film, and return to the oven for further 5 minutes to cook the centre. Remove from the oven and cool on a wire rack.

Filling

- 1½ cups macadamia nut pieces, toasted
- 1 cup sugar
- 85g butter, melted
- ¾ teaspoon salt
- 6 size 7 eggs
- 425g liquid glucose (corn syrup or maltose)
- 1 lemon, zested

Scatter the macadamia nuts evenly into the pre-baked tart case.

Preheat the oven to 140°C.

In a mixing bowl, beat the sugar, butter and salt together until soft and creamy. Add in the eggs, two at a time, mixing well between each addition. Add in the glucose and lemon zest; beat well.

Pour the mixture into the tart base and bake for 50 minutes or until just set.

Ginger beer
crème brûlée

Makes 14 Chinese custard cups (can be
purchased at an Asian supermarket)

2 x 375ml	ginger beer
3 knobs	fresh ginger, peeled and grated
½ cup	raw sugar
2 cups	cream
2 cups	milk
1	vanilla bean, split down the middle (or 1 teaspoon pure vanilla essence)
10	egg yolks
½ cup	raw sugar
1 teaspoon	salt
14 tablespoons	caster sugar

Place the ginger beer, grated ginger and the first
measure of raw sugar into a saucepan and reduce it
down until a quarter cup of syrup remains (about
15 minutes).

Meanwhile, bring the cream, milk and vanilla to a
near boil.

While this is happening, lightly cream the egg yolks
with the second measure of raw sugar.

Whisk the cream liquid into the egg mixture
then this mixture into the ginger syrup, whisking
together for a few seconds. Try not to overwhisk
and make it foamy. Add the salt and taste.

Preheat the oven to 140°C.

Place the custard cups into a deep roasting dish
lined with a tea towel. (The cloth will diffuse
the bottom heat from the oven and regulate the
temperature.)

Pull the oven rack out, place the roasting tray on
the rack and fill the cups to the top.

Pour in boiling water in the oven tray to halfway
up the cups and bake for 50 minutes.

Once baked, remove crème brûlées from the tray;
place into a refrigerator to set (up to 6 hours).

To serve, sprinkle the surface of each brûlée with
1 tablespoon of caster sugar and caramelise with a
blow torch. If you don't have a blow torch, hammer
flat a spoon that will fit the inside the cup (choose
one you no longer need!), bend the handle to a 90°
angle, place into a gas flame until red hot and dab
onto the sugar.

Great with biscotti and coconut sorbet.

Coconut sorbet

¾ cup	caster sugar
1 cup	water
¼	cinnamon stick
½	orange, peeled
1 cup	coconut cream

Place the sugar and water into a saucepan, bring to the boil. Add the cinnamon and orange peel, simmer for 3 minutes, stirring occasionally.

Remove from the heat, and stir in the coconut cream and leave to cool.

Push the liquid through a fine sieve with the back of a ladle and discard the cinnamon but keep the peel.

Julienne the peel and add back into the mixture.

Churn in an ice-cream maker and freeze, or freeze in thin layers on trays. Scoop up the frozen mixture and blitz in a liquidiser and re-freeze.

As I have travelled and worked in various countries, I have noticed each place seems to have its own particular signature dishes. In Sydney it was barbecued baby octopus salad and sticky toffee pudding; in New York it was miso-blackened fish and tomatillo salsa; and in New Zealand it was pumpkin soup and crème brûlée. Crème brûlées sell like hotcakes; diners love to crack through the sugar chard sitting on top of the custard. At one stage at Pure Tastes, they were almost a culinary swear word in the kitchen, we were so completely over making them! But diners demanded we keep them on the menu. I thought back to the days my grandmother had ginger beer brewing in the pantry, bubbling and often exploding. This memory inspired the flavour of this recipe as it became both our restaurant and out-catering signature dish.

Penang curry

Serves 8

Fresh paste base

3	red chillies, chopped
2	shallots, peeled and chopped
2	garlic cloves, peeled and sliced
2	coriander roots and stems, chopped
1 teaspoon	salt
1 tablespoon	curry powder
2 tablespoons	water

In a food processor or pestle and mortar, pulverise the ingredients to a paste. Place into an airtight container, cover with a layer of vegetable oil and refrigerate until required.

As a chef, my profile gained some momentum whilst I was working at Shells Restaurant in Tairua on the Coromandel Peninsula. The summer and autumn months are truly spectacular with the pristine eastern beaches nestled in bush and the western coastline lined with pohutukawa trees heavy with red blossom. In winter though, the huge rainfall and cooler weather mean that something warming and rustic is called for. Some of our regular clientele were vegetarian, the infamous forgotten diner. I had this Malaysian curry recipe that needed a bit of reconstruction to become a zesty, well-balanced curry that could not only feature vegetables but also chicken, pork or wood-smoked salmon. It's great to share with friends on a stormy night.

Curry

¼ cup	vegetable oil
2	dried chillies
4	garlic cloves, finely chopped
1 recipe	fresh curry paste
2 tablespoons	sugar
1 teaspoon	salt
¼ cup	light soy sauce
2 cups	vegetable stock
2 cups	coconut cream
½ cup	coriander roots, stem and leaves, chopped
¼ cup	basil leaves, shredded
2	lemons, juiced

In a wok or heavy-based saucepan, heat the vegetable oil. Add the dried chillies, garlic and curry paste and cook until it darkens slightly and smells aromatic. Add the sugar and salt. Add the soy sauce, stock and coconut cream. Bring to the boil, reduce the heat and simmer until the curry thickens (about 10 minutes).

Remove from the heat and place curry into a liquidiser. Add in the herbs and lemon juice and blend until smooth.

This curry freezes well.

Serve with steamed jasmine rice, Greek yoghurt and fresh lime wedges.

Indigenous dukkah

Makes 750g

375g	white sesame seeds, toasted and divided into two portions
½ cup	hazelnuts, roasted and skinned
¼ cup	pistachio kernels, lightly toasted
¼ cup	sunflower seeds, toasted
2 tablespoons	flaxseeds (optional)
3 teaspoons	sea salt
3 tablespoons	cumin seeds, toasted and ground
1 teaspoon	black peppercorns, toasted and ground
1 tablespoon	horopito herb (optional)

In a food processor, process half the sesame seeds. Place in a mixing bowl with the remaining sesame seeds.

In the food processor, pulse the hazelnuts and pistachio until kibbled in texture. Add these nuts and the remaining ingredients to the sesame seeds and toss together.

Place the dukkah into an airtight container. It can be stored for up to 2–3 months.

During my time in Sydney in the early 1990s, I would walk to work in Darlinghurst past Turkish and Middle Eastern cafés. I stared through their windows at wonderful dishes and enjoyed the incredible aromas. One of the very first dishes I discovered was a watermelon, date and feta salad with freshly chopped coriander and this sprinkling of aromatic seeds and nuts. When I returned to New Zealand, diners thought it very peculiar that I sprinkled dukkah over salads and didn't just serve it with bread and olive oil like everybody else.

There are many dukkah products on the market. Some are not well made — manufacturers get trapped into adding dried herbs and make the dukkah with too fine a texture. This recipe embraces Maori herbs whilst staying true to its natural origin. It is so popular that John from Skellon Foods, Auckland, gave me the task of knocking out 8kg of it at a time for them to sell, so it is fair to say I have had lots of practice at making this aromatic dry dip.

Chocolate

Cacao trees grow within 20 degrees of the equator because they need about 2000 millimetres of rainfall a year, and a temperature range of between 21°C and 32°C. The bean of the cacao tree has an intensely bitter taste, and must be fermented to develop the flavour. After fermentation, the beans are dried, cleaned, roasted, and the shell is removed to produce cacao nibs. The nibs are then ground and liquified, resulting in pure chocolate liquid. This liquid is further processed into cocoa solids and cocoa butter.

The finest plain dark chocolate couvertures contain at least 70 per cent cocoa (solids and butter), while milk chocolate usually contains up to 50 per cent cocoa. High-quality white chocolate couvertures contain only about 33 per cent cocoa.

Yes, chocolate is sexy and will make you go weak at the knees! Valentine's Day, Easter and Christmas wouldn't be the same without it. Cooking chocolate can be challenging and will test your patience, as it is susceptible to changes in temperature. It wouldn't be at all strange to find me shaving chocolate curls in a temperature-controlled wine room, or using chocolate liqueur to stabilise melted chocolate before adding whipped cream.

I once held a Christmas party for some real food lovers, walking encyclopedias of culinary knowledge — diners we just love to entertain. We served them a five-course set menu, and I announced the dish and the wine match before each course. When it came to dessert, I wanted the guests to tell me what they were eating, mentioning that they needed to think outside the square. I waited until a good amount of dessert had been eaten, then asked the question. Caramel trifle was one suggestion. The answer: a Greek-style roasted eggplant and chocolate tiramisu, laced with mascarpone and caramel. There was stunned silence followed by comments like 'this chef must be on another planet!' The dish tasted fantastic but it had taken them outside their comfort zone. If it was on an à la carte menu, diners would bypass it and order something safe — a lemon tart or sticky date pudding.

The diners had all seen chocolate in a new light — and eggplant too for that matter!

Grandma's chocolate whisky pudding

Makes a 20cm pudding

50g	butter, chopped and at room temperature
½ cup	caster sugar
1	egg, beaten
1 teaspoon	whisky
1 cup	flour
1 teaspoon	baking powder
½ teaspoon	salt
2 tablespoons	cocoa powder
⅓ cup	milk
1 tablespoon	cocoa powder
½ cup	sugar
1½ cups	hot water

Preheat the oven to 150°C.

In a mixing bowl, cream the butter and sugar together until light and fluffy. Add in the egg and whisky, beating well. Sieve in the flour, baking powder and salt, and fold into the butter mixture. Dissolve the first measure of cocoa in milk and fold through the mixture.

Pour into a greased nonstick tin. Sprinkle the surface with the remaining cocoa powder and sugar. Carefully pour the hot water over mixture. Place into the oven and bake for 45 minutes.

I spent much of my school holidays with my grandmother in her kitchen, baking cookies, helping make preserves and having a good old time making a complete mess everywhere. One of her quick treats when family dropped in unexpectedly was to whip up this very easy and satisfying self-saucing chocolate pudding. I remember her collecting the cream off the top of the milk, delivered in those days in glass pint bottles, and serving this with the pudding along with fresh boysenberries picked in the late afternoon from her garden.

Quivering white chocolate tart

Makes a 26cm tart

Chocolate tart base

360g	butter, diced
150g	icing sugar, sifted
4	egg yolks
50ml	cream
425g	plain flour
75g	Dutch cocoa powder
a pinch	salt
1	egg white, lightly beaten

In a cake mixer, cream the butter with the paddle attachment. Add in the icing sugar and mix briefly. Whisk the egg yolks and cream together; work into the butter.

With the mixer on slow speed, add the flour, cocoa and salt into the butter in two amounts, allowing it to be well mixed between each addition.

Refrigerate for 2 hours. (This dough also freezes well.)

Preheat the oven to 170°C.

Wipe the bench with a damp cloth. Spread two overlapped sheets of cling film on the bench. Scatter the area with flour, place down the dough, flatten and scatter with more flour. Place two more overlapped sheets over the dough and roll out to 3mm thick.

Remove the top layer of cling film, invert into the springform tin and push down into the corners with the remaining cling film.

Two-thirds fill the tin with baking beans, lentils or rice and bake for 15 minutes. Take out of the oven.

Remove the baking beans, and return to the oven for a further 5 minutes to cook the bottom.

Remove from the oven and brush the inside of the tart shell with the egg white to create a lacquer.

Cool in the tin on a wire rack for 20 minutes or so.

Continued overleaf

White chocolate filling

4	gelatine leaves (or 1 teaspoon gelatine powder)
1¾ cups	cream
1¼ cups	milk
835g	white chocolate couverture buttons
8	eggs, beaten
1 tablespoon	white chocolate crème de cacao liqueur (optional)
¾ teaspoon	salt

Preheat the oven to 130°C.

Soak the gelatine leaves in cold water until limp and soft or alternatively soak the gelatine powder in a tablespoon of cold water then heat in the microwave until it turns to a liquid.

In a saucepan, bring the cream and milk to a boil. Whisk in the white chocolate, and mix until melted and combined.

Whisk the chocolate mixture into the beaten eggs then pass through a fine sieve into a clean bowl. Whisk in the squeezed gelatine leaves or dissolved powdered gelatine. Whisk in the liqueur and salt.

Pour the mixture into the tart case and bake for 1 hour and 15 minutes until set.

Remove from the oven and cool for 15 minutes before loosening from the tin. It will keep in the refrigerator for two weeks, or you can freeze it for up to a month.

To serve, warm a wedge of tart in a preheated 200°C oven for 1½ minutes and serve with hokey pokey ice cream and seasonal fruit.

I have always admired high achievers who come out of retirement to continue their professional life and again show their true magic, such as Joël Robuchon, once proclaimed as one of the best chefs in the world. Every Michelin-starred chef makes a dark chocolate tart, usually a take on someone else's, left to bake in a turned-off oven. Joël was famous for his extraordinary tart, baked with the oven still turned on, cooled, then a slice reheated so it just quivered. I hadn't heard of anyone trying to make a white chocolate tart like this but after two weeks of failures in the kitchen, I struck gold and it became my signature tart — inspired by this talented French chef and his amazing insight.

Kiwi chocolate carrot cake

Makes a 26cm cake

275g	butter, softened
3 teaspoons	orange zest
1 cup	caster sugar
3	eggs, beaten
1½ tablespoons	golden syrup
3	large carrots, peeled and grated
1½ cups	self-raising flour
¾ teaspoon	baking soda
¼ cup	cocoa powder
1 cup + 2 tablespoons	milk

Grease a 26cm springform tin, then line with baking paper to sit 5cm higher than the top of the tin. Preheat the oven to 165°C.

In a mixing bowl, cream the butter, sugar and zest until just combined. Beat in the eggs and golden syrup.

Combine the dry ingredients together and stir into the egg mixture in two batches along with the carrot and milk.

Pour mixture into prepared tin and bake for 70 minutes.

Remove from the oven and stand in the tin for 5 minutes before turning out onto a cooling rack.

Growing up and cooking with my grandma, the making of delicious cakes and cookies was often the best part of my day. Tugging on her apron strings, requesting the spatula to lick, my face would be smeared with chocolate batter and my T-shirt covered in flour. Every house and coffee shop in New Zealand has a version of a chocolate or carrot cake. Here's one from my dear friend Annie, who is a baking genius, throwing together ingredients without recipes — her moist cake is legendary, just like Grandma's.

Fastest chocolate dessert ever!

Makes 1 litre

Chocolate granita

3 cups	caster sugar
2½ cups	water
2 tablespoons	dark crème de cacao liqueur
1 tablespoon	Dutch cocoa powder
1 tablespoon	liquid glucose
2½ cups	water

In a saucepan, bring the sugar and the first measure of water to the boil, simmer until slightly syrupy. Remove from the heat.

Meanwhile, in a mixing bowl, mix the liqueur, cocoa powder and glucose together with the second measure of water. Whisk in the sugar syrup.

Pour the mixture into several shallow trays, place in the freezer until almost frozen. With a spoon scrape the granita into frozen chards (flakes of ice) and refreeze. Once frozen again, gather into an airtight container and keep in the freezer until required.

Chocolate sauce

1 cup	water
140g	caster sugar
¼ cup	liquid glucose
¼ cup	Dutch cocoa powder
¼ cup	dark chocolate buttons
¼ teaspoon	salt

In a saucepan, add in the water, sugar and glucose and bring to the boil.

Remove a quarter cup of the liquid and place into a bowl.

Whisk in the Dutch cocoa to make a paste and whisk this back into the remaining syrup.

Whisk in the chocolate buttons until melted and simmer for 3 minutes.

Pass the sauce through a fine conical sieve (also called a chinois sieve) and whisk in the salt.

Assembly

Place serving glasses in the freezer for at least 2 hours. Place a scoop of vanilla ice cream in each glass, pour over a hot short black coffee (espresso), 2 tablespoons of chocolate sauce, a spoonful of chocolate granita crumble and some crushed Maltesers. Serve with long parfait spoons.

Chefs are always reprimanded for making recipes too complicated for the home cook. This magic dish was inspired by the Italian fresh coffee dessert affogato. I was filming as one of chefs on the *April in the Afternoon* show on the Living Channel when this chocolate granita idea sprang into my head. Fellow chef Chris Hagan and I accidentally discovered while making this recipe that shaved chocolate ice is not only easy to make, but tastes outstanding and feels amazing in the mouth. Yum!

Berries

Berry growing was one of the first horticultural industries to be established in New Zealand. The demand for jam fruit peaked in the early 1900s with large areas of raspberries and strawberries being grown in Nelson, Central Otago, Canterbury and the Wairarapa.

Raspberries are grown chiefly in the South Island, mostly in Nelson and Canterbury. Strawberries are grown in both islands, mainly in the specialised growing areas of Auckland and South Canterbury. Blackcurrants tend to be found in Canterbury and Wellington. Commercial gooseberry production is almost entirely limited to Wellington.

My grandmother would send me out to pick berries while her homemade pavlova rested on the windowsill in the afternoon. I'm sure she wondered why her grandson would take so long to pick the small amount of berries I returned with, although the smears of dried red juice on my face probably gave it away! I have always had a passion for berries — I often made the hour-long drive to gather raspberries in Otaki, north of Wellington to serve with my honey wafers with passionfruit curd, a delicious and eye-catching dessert. The berries themselves are wonderful to photograph: behind the lens, fine hairs protrude, bubbles of flesh glisten and the bright colours of summer beckon.

Blueberry and almond friands

Makes 15

260g	butter, melted
375g	ground almonds
360g	egg whites (approximately 11 eggs), lightly beaten
3 teaspoons	vanilla extract
560g	icing sugar, sifted
185g	plain flour, sifted
1½ cups	blueberries (if frozen, defrost and drain first)

Butter and flour the small oval-shaped friand moulds. (Alternatively, you can use medium-sized muffin trays.)

Preheat the oven to 160°C.

In a mixing bowl, combine all the ingredients except the blueberries and mix together.

Spoon the batter halfway up the moulds, dig a little hole and put in some blueberries. Top up with batter and place a few blueberries on top.

Put into the oven and bake for 30 minutes or until cooked.

Cool in the moulds on a rack for 10 minutes before turning out.

Dust with icing sugar and serve warm with thick Greek-style yoghurt.

Kiwis love muffins, and it was very tempting to include a perfect berry muffin recipe in this book. But this recipe, by far the best for using blueberries, kept tugging away at my mind. At Pure Tastes in Kerikeri we would source our fresh organic blueberries from Omaha Beach, a vibrant wine-growing region northeast of Auckland. These lovely, moist oval French teacakes just explode in the mouth.

Raspberries, honey wafers and passionfruit curd

Serves 6

Honey wafers

60g	butter, softened
80g	icing sugar, sifted
60ml	liquid honey
80g	plain flour, sieved
1 teaspoon	ginger powder
70g	egg whites (approximately 2 large egg whites)
½ cup	macadamias, lightly pulsed in a food processor

Take a baking sheet, spray with oil, line with nonstick baking paper.

In a food processor, cream the butter with the icing sugar. Add in the honey then the flour mixed with the ginger powder. With the motor running, add in the egg whites in a slow, steady stream.

Scoop out the batter into a bowl and refrigerate for 2 hours before using. The batter will last for 1 month when refrigerated.

Preheat the oven to 160°C.

Make a template for the wafers by taking a plastic ice-cream container lid and cutting out a 90mm circle with a sharp knife. The template is the central round hole.

Place the template on a non-stick tray lined with baking paper, spread an even, thin layer of batter

in the circle, lift up and repeat until the tray is full. Scatter over some macadamia nuts.

Bake in the oven until golden brown all over (about 8–10 minutes).

Remove straightaway from the tray with the back of a fish slice and place on a flat surface to cool and become crisp.

Continued overleaf

Passionfruit curd

6	egg yolks (preferably free range)
100g	caster sugar
1	lime, zested
100ml	passionfruit pulp, seeds strained and all but 3 tablespoons discarded
130g	butter, chopped
3 tablespoons	passionfruit seeds, reserved from passionfruit pulp

In a mixing bowl, whisk the egg yolks with the caster sugar and lime zest until light and creamy. Whisk in the passionfruit pulp and place the bowl over a saucepan of simmering water. Toss in half the butter and stir as it starts to thicken. Add the remaining butter and stir until amalgamated.

Pass the curd through a sieve into a clean bowl and stir in the passionfruit seeds. Refrigerate until cold and set.

Assembly

½ cup	mascarpone cheese
4 punnets	raspberries

To serve, fold the mascarpone through the passionfruit curd.

In the centre of a plate, place one wafer and arrange some raspberries on it. Place a spoonful of passionfruit curd and top with another wafer, gently pressing down.

Repeat with raspberries and curd, top with another wafer and serve.

This dish is often misnamed *mille-feuille*, French for 'thousand leaves', on restaurant menus, when in fact there aren't a thousand layers as in puff pastry. Making the layers requires just a little time and patience. Store them in an airtight container with either a silica pad from a used nori packet or a piece of new chalk to absorb the moisture and keep the wafers crisp until needed. This is a knockout dessert which is easy to assemble for a dinner party.

Vanilla latte cotto with blackberries

Makes 6

375ml	milk
125ml	cream
1½	lemons, zested
½	vanilla bean, chopped
125g	egg whites (approximately 4 eggs)
200g	sugar
200g	amaretti biscuits
30	blackberries
150ml	cream, lightly beaten

Buy a piece of downpipe 9cm in diameter and 20cm long, and have it cut into 2cm rings.

The night before serving, in a saucepan warm the milk, cream, lemon zest and vanilla together and cool. Place in the refrigerator overnight to infuse.

Gently whisk the egg whites and sugar together, pass through a sieve into a bowl and refrigerate.

Whisk the vanilla cream into the egg whites and put into a pouring jug.

Cover the base of each ring with 2 squares of cling film and secure with a rubber band.

Bring water to a simmer in a wide steamer, place the rings into the insert of the steamer and fill the moulds to the top of the rings. Turn the heat to low, cover with a lid and cook for approximately 25 minutes until set but still slightly wobbly.

If you have a bells and whistles combi oven, cook the rings on steam mode, 85°C for 35 minutes at half fan speed.

Refrigerate the latte cotto until cold then serve with crumbled amaretti biscuits, blackberries and cream.

A restaurant is always trying to find ways to use up egg whites, often freezing them until needed. My good friend and the opening chef at Pure Tastes, Simun Dragicevich, told me about these egg-white custards he used to make in Sydney in a special oven with all the bells and whistles. We didn't have one of these ovens so, after a week of trial and error, I remodelled this recipe to be cooked in a steamer. The vanilla notes partner beautifully with tart blackberries and whipped cream.

Strawberry rosemary shortcake

Serves 8

White chocolate rosemary shortcake

2	eggs
85g	caster sugar
1 tablespoon	rosemary leaves, chopped
150g	white chocolate buttons, melted
60g	butter, diced
1 teaspoon	vanilla extract
105g	plain flour
½ teaspoon	salt

Preheat the oven to 155°C. Line a deep-sided tray with nonstick baking paper.

In a mixing bowl, whisk the eggs until light and fluffy. Add in the sugar and rosemary, whisk until thick.

Add the butter to the melted white chocolate and stir in the vanilla.

Fold the chocolate mixture into the egg mixture. Fold in the flour and salt.

Place into the oven and bake for 35 minutes. Remove and cool on a wire rack.

Cut the shortcake to the size of parfait moulds and store between pieces of baking paper in an airtight container until needed.

The strawberry is the queen of all berries, mouth-smacking and meaty. At a catering event for a long lunch in Paihia, Bay of Islands, this recipe was designed with a play on shortcake with a modern twist. A velvety iced parfait sits on top of the shortcake with strawberries tossed in dark balsamic vinegar and topped with fried rosemary leaves. Either of these components is great by itself but they partner beautifully with the mystery of rosemary.

White chocolate parfait

6	egg yolks
20g	caster sugar
120g	white chocolate buttons, melted
2	egg whites
240ml	cream, whipped
70ml	white crème de cacao liqueur
½ teaspoon	salt
1 cup	white chocolate, chopped
3 punnets	strawberries, trimmed with a small knife
2 tablespoons	dark balsamic vinegar
6 tablespoons	berry coulis (thin berry purée)
4 tablespoons	rosemary leaves, crisped in olive oil

Take 8 downpipe rings (see the latte cotto recipe on the previous page), cover the base of each ring with 2 squares of cling film, secure with a rubber band and place onto a flat tray.

In a mixing bowl, whisk the yolks with 10g caster sugar. In another clean mixing bowl, whisk the egg whites with the remaining 10g caster sugar to a stiff meringue.

Gently combine the yolks, chocolate, meringue, cream and liqueur. Spoon the mixture halfway up the moulds and freeze overnight.

In a mixing bowl, toss the strawberries, balsamic vinegar and berry coulis around to coat.

To assemble, place a piece of shortcake at room temperature in the middle of a plate. Place an unmoulded parfait onto the shortcake. Arrange the strawberries on top of the parfait, drizzle over the remaining coulis and scatter with crispy rosemary leaves and serve.

Citrus fruit

It is so satisfying to pick citrus fruit at the end of the day, still warm from the sun. Slice it open and juice pours out with the gentlest squeeze.

Citrus fruit grows in abundance in the subtropical climate of the Far North. As most of the fruit is exported, you need to have an ear to the ground and visit the farmers' markets to source the best fruit. Luckily, two of my regular restaurant clients, Rhona and Marcel, own a citrus orchard, Lemon Fresh, in Waipapa. Their fruit is destined for my stove and that Kiwi favourite, lemon meringue pie.

Citrus fruits release far more juice if they are kept at room temperature, except for easy-peel mandarins, which need to be refrigerated. If you encounter a few thick-skinned specimens, knead them on a hard surface before cutting. When craving the ultimate gin and tonic, cut the lime or lemon in half (or try a grapefruit), insert a fork and twist to release a little flesh as well as the juice, cut the squeezed piece into four and put a couple of pieces into a glass loaded with crushed ice.

Moroccan artichoke and lemon dip

Makes 1 litre

750g	cooked and drained globe artichoke hearts, cut in quarters
3	large onions, cut in half and roasted in their skins
8	garlic cloves, peeled and chopped
small knob	fresh ginger, peeled and grated
2 tablespoons	American mustard
4	lemons, juiced
1 teaspoon	turmeric powder
1 teaspoon	cumin, ground
½ teaspoon	cinnamon quills, ground
½ teaspoon	cardamom seeds, ground
2 tablespoons	brown sugar
1½ cups	olive oil
2 teaspoons	salt

Heat the solid grill plate of the barbecue until smoking hot.

Drizzle over some olive oil, brown the pieces of artichoke in batches, placing them into a large mixing bowl as you go.

Peel the onions and chop into small pieces and mix through the artichokes.

Mix in the remaining ingredients except the olive oil and salt and blend in a food processor until smooth.

With a spatula, remove the mixture from the food processor and place half of it into a blender or liquidiser.

Start the motor and add in half the olive oil and blend till smooth, empty and repeat the process with the second half.

Push this dip through a sieve, adjust the flavour with salt and extra lemon juice if needed.

Serve with crusty sourdough bread and cheese as a dip or thin down to make a dressing to use with fish or chicken.

People seem daunted by the spiky flower of the globe artichoke. Every season, artichokes with shaved spearlike stems tend to arrive on my doorstep anonymously, waiting to be bottled. The globe artichoke is not everyone's cup of tea, and I desperately wanted to launch this thistle into stardom. As the head chef at Paramount in Auckland, I created this dip with lemon and Moroccan spices, which we served with freshly baked fougasse bread. By the way, there is no doubt I will have you operating a spice grinder by the time you've read this book!

Lemon meringue pie

Makes a 26cm pie

Malt biscuit base

320g	malt biscuits
½ teaspoon	salt
150g	butter, melted

In a food processor, blitz the biscuits and salt into crumbs, pouring the butter in through the opening. Using a spoon, scoop out the crumbs and press down around the sides of the nonstick springform tin. If you have an espresso machine, use the coffee tamper to pack down your base, otherwise use a sturdy glass.

Place in the refrigerator to harden for about 1 hour.

Lemon curd filling

¾ cup	lemon juice
¾ cup	caster sugar
250g	butter, diced
8	size 7 eggs
¾ cup	caster sugar
3	gelatine leaves, soaked in cold water till limp or 1 teaspoon powdered gelatine

In a saucepan, place the lemon juice, the first lot of caster sugar and the butter, then bring to the boil.

Meanwhile, take a stainless steel bowl and put in the eggs and the remaining caster sugar and beat until light and creamy.

Whisk the boiling juice into the egg mixture, whisking constantly, then return the mixture to the saucepan. Stir constantly over a medium heat until the mixture thickens but does not boil.

If using leaf gelatine, squeeze the water from the gelatine and whisk into your lemon curd until dissolved. If using powdered gelatine, mix with a tablespoon of water, heat in a microwave for a few seconds until dissolved then add to the lemon curd.

Pass the mixture through a fine sieve and adjust the taste with a pinch of salt if required to bring out the lemon flavour.

Pour the filling on top of the biscuit base and refrigerate for 2 hours.

Continued overleaf

Ultimate meringue

5	egg whites at room temperature
pinch	salt
½ cup	caster sugar
1	lemon, zested
½ cup	caster sugar

Preheat the oven to 150°C.

Place the egg whites and salt in a cake mixer and beat until soft peaks form. With the mixer in motion, sprinkle in the first measure of the sugar and whisk until the egg whites are firm. Sprinkle in the second measure of sugar mixed with lemon zest and continue to whisk until firm and glossy (about 3 minutes).

Take a hot, dry spoon and scoop small egg-shaped balls (quenelles) of meringue and place on top of the chilled lemon curd filling. Place into the oven to bake for about 20 minutes until the meringue is lightly golden in patches.

Cool for 2 hours. Remove from the pan and serve dusted with icing sugar.

Although it plays second fiddle to the pavlova in the popularity stakes, this dish is surely a favourite of nearly every New Zealander. I remember being four years old, watching my grandma's lemon meringue pie cooling on the windowsill of her house in Whakatane. My grandma watches with amusement as she offers me a morsel, my face stunned in silence as I experience the tartness of the lemon curd and the sweetness of the toasted marshmallow meringue. Heaven!

Fried orange, tamarind and coconut mussels

Serves 4

1 knob	fresh ginger, peeled and sliced thinly
6	garlic cloves, peeled and sliced thinly
3	oranges, peel and juice
1	red onion, peeled and sliced thinly
⅓ cup	peanut oil
1 tablespoon	green Thai curry paste
¾ cup	tamarind pulp
2	lemons, juiced
2 cups	fish or chicken stock
40	unopened mussels, beards removed with a tea towel
½ cup	raw sugar
400ml can	coconut cream
1 tablespoon	coriander leaves and stems, chopped roughly
1 tablespoon	mint leaves, chopped roughly (I recommend Thai mint)
1 tablespoon	basil leaves, chopped roughly (I recommend Thai basil)

Heat a little vegetable oil in a wok, and stir-fry the ginger, garlic, orange peel and red onion until golden. Drain on a paper towel to cool.

Heat the peanut oil in a thick-bottomed saucepan. Add in the Thai curry paste and fry with the help of a wooden spoon till fragrant (it will darken slightly).

Add in the tamarind and fruit juices, bring back to the boil. Pour in the stock and bring back to the boil. Add in the ginger, garlic, orange and onion.

Add in the mussels, cover with a lid and steam in the juice until just starting to open (about 4 minutes).

Add in the raw sugar, coconut cream and picked herbs and bring to the boil then simmer for 2 more minutes.

With kitchen tongs, remove the mussels and place into a serving bowl, keeping the liquid in the saucepan. Increase the heat and rapidly reduce the broth by a third.

Pour the broth over the mussels and serve with some steamed jasmine rice and lemon finger bowls.

My love for Thai food was influenced by David Thompson of Darley Street Thai in Sydney. He is a master of flavours, wonderful textures and soul-searching ingredients.

Personally I find it hard to get creative with New Zealand green-lipped mussels. During my time as head chef at The Cathedral, a Parnell eatery in Auckland, I discovered that mussels team up well with the sweet and sour flavour of tamarind. I gave this aromatic dish the push onto the menu and boy, did it sell!

Orange, cashew and caramel semifreddo

Makes 2 loaves

Butterscotch

1 cup	caster sugar
1 cup	water
1 cup	cream
½ cup	unsalted butter, diced

In a saucepan, always put the sugar in first, followed by the water. Place on a high heat and stir until the mixture is a deep caramel but do not burn or the sauce will be bitter.

Whisk in the cream and butter, and simmer until a smooth, thick sauce is achieved. Cool before using.

Orange semifreddo

1 cup	toasted cashew nut pieces
9	egg yolks
¾ cup	caster sugar
½ cup	butterscotch liqueur
1 tablespoon	lemon juice
1	orange, zested
2 tablespoons	candied orange peel, finely chopped
1¼ cups	cream, whipped

Spray 2 loaf tins with oil and lay a sheet of cling film on the bottom and sides, pushing down into the tins. Scatter a third of the cashew nuts over the bottom and a little of the butterscotch sauce.

In a stainless-steel mixing bowl, beat the yolks and sugar until lemon-coloured. Whisk in the butterscotch liqueur and lemon juice.

Place the bowl over simmering water and continue to whip constantly until the mixture is light and covers the back of a spoon (a sabayon).

Remove from the heat and whisk over a bowl of iced water and continue to whip until cold. Fold in the orange zest and candied peel, followed by the cream.

Spoon in enough mixture to fill each tin halfway, scatter over another third of the cashew nuts and spoon over some of the butterscotch sauce.

Fill to the top of the tins with the mixture, scatter over the remaining cashews and spoon over some more of the butterscotch sauce. Tap the tins on the bench and fold over the cling film to seal.

Place into the freezer overnight then turn out, peel off the cling film and cut into sliced portions. Serve with diced mango.

I love to demonstrate and champion all things culinary — it's the part of my profession I most enjoy. In Waimate North at New Zealand's oldest Pastoral and Industrial Show, the 'Savouring the Source' cooking stage is a popular destination. The group of chefs inspires the audience by using products available from the supermarket to create delicious recipes that are easy to prepare at home. I made a dish using Tatua's new ice-cream mix which was a real hit! I used the mix as a base for an Italian semifreddo, made without an ice-cream maker and frozen in a loaf tin. Organisers found it difficult to shift the audience on; everyone loves icecream and they all wanted to have a taste . . .

Conversion tables

Conversions are to the nearest round number.

Abbreviations

ml	=	millilitre	cm	=	centimetre
g	=	gram	mm	=	millimetre
kg	=	kilogram	°C	=	degrees Celsius

New Zealand metric measures

1 teaspoon	=	5ml
1 tablespoon	=	15ml (= 3 teaspoons)
1 cup	=	250ml
2 cups	=	500ml
4 cups	=	1 litre

Grams to ounces

25g	=	1oz
100g	=	3.5oz
200g	=	7oz
450g	=	16oz (= 1lb)
1kg	=	1000g = 2lb 4oz

Oven temperatures

140°C	=	275°F
150°C	=	300°F
160°C	=	325°F
180°C	=	350°F
200°C	=	400°F

Liquid measures

125ml	=	4 fluid oz	=	½ cup
250ml	=	8 fluid oz	=	1 cup
1000ml	=	1¾ pints	=	4 cups

Before and after measures

100g cheese	=	1 cup grated cheese
200g (2) potatoes	=	1 cup mashed potato
⅓ cup uncooked rice	=	1 cup cooked rice
4 slices toast bread	=	1 cup fresh crumbs
⅓ cup uncooked pasta	=	1 cup cooked pasta

Other useful information

1 cup self-raising flour	=	1 cup plain flour, 1 tablespoon baking powder and ¼ teaspoon salt
1 gelatine leaf	=	½ teaspoon powdered gelatine
1 egg white	=	32g

Fan-forced temperatures are approximately 20°C hotter than normal. As a general rule 180°C fan-bake is the same as 200°C standard-bake. This will vary slightly depending on the oven.

Pantry of
ingredients

www.barkers.co.nz

www.barkersfruit.biz

Barker's started as a small family business and is now a leading New Zealand-owned food manufacturer. They offer a wide range of great-tasting condiments suitable for both the home kitchen and the hospitality industry. I am very proud to be part of their product development team.

www.firstdrop.co.nz

This superb olive oil is grown almost in my backyard. It's from the subtropical Far North district where the olives are picked and pressed to make superlative extra-virgin olive oil, often pressed earlier than in any other part of New Zealand. Together we launched my beautiful parmesan-infused olive oil that features in this book.

www.lemonfresh.co.nz

I find Lemon Fresh Pantry Essentials an easy, accessible, affordable range of lemon ingredients. Their lemon juice, zest and preserved lemons can be used in any of the recipes in my book that call for the natural zesty flavour of lemons.

www.beeflambnz.co.nz

Beef and Lamb New Zealand is responsible for promotion from pasture to plate of beef and sheep meat throughout the country. No matter where I've been in the world I've always found New Zealand beef and lamb to be the best. Check out the useful diners' directory of restaurants that carry the current Hallmarks of Excellence Award on the website.

www.gourmetdirect.com

Gourmet Direct have supplied quality meats, poultry and game birds to many of the restaurants I have worked in. These are now available to the home cook through their door-to-door delivery service which I thoroughly recommend. They supplied product to our visiting chefs and demonstrators when I operated Pure Tastes cooking school.

www.mightymushrooms.co.nz

Family owned and operated, Mighty Mushrooms grow and supply the best gourmet oyster mushrooms to chefs, retailers, restaurants and the general public throughout Northland and the rest of New Zealand.

www.delica.co.nz

Delica is an international produce marketer. It exports a wide range of fruit and vegetables from New Zealand, Australia and South America to markets all over the globe. Main lines are apples, citrus, table grapes, berries and stonefruit.

Honeysuckle Grove Orchards

476 Kerikeri Road, RD3, Kerikeri, Northland, phone 09 407 8471, fax 09 407 6471, email: gordonbeale@actrix.co.nz

Gordon Beale at Honeysuckle Grove Orchards in Kerikeri grows some of the best vegetables around and can grow to order with advance notice. Produce is often shipped outside Northland to top chefs such as Simon Gault.

www.regalsalmon.co.nz

Regal Marlborough Salmon is a brand of the New Zealand King Salmon Company. They own and operate all stages of farming, production and marketing of their salmon, and offer a consistent supply of fresh and smoked salmon all year round. Their fabulous products can be found in supermarkets throughout New Zealand.

Tricks of
the trade

Keep mesclun lettuce greens crisp for longer by spinning and storing in a salad spinner in the refrigerator.

Separate egg white from the yolk by passing the egg through clean fingers into a bowl.

Maximise the volume of whipped egg whites by using egg whites at room temperature or warmed to 37°C in a saucepan.

Knead citrus fruit or warm it in a microwave for 15 seconds for easier juicing.

Use a wide metal speed peeler to remove seeds from pumpkin or squash, and to peel rind from citrus fruit. The end can also be used to scale fish.

For better colouring, coat meat or fish with cooking oil rather than heating the oil in a nonstick sauté pan.

Peel an avocado by cutting it in half, removing the stone with the heel of a knife and scooping out the flesh with a large spoon.

Keep potatoes from sprouting by placing an apple in their bag.

When hard-boiling an egg, add a teaspoon of salt to the water before cooking for easier peeling.

Remove burnt-on food from a sauté pan by adding a drop or two of dishwashing liquid to enough water to cover the bottom of the pan and bringing the mixture to the boil.

Stop a tart case from seeping its liquid contents by brushing beaten egg white on the inside while hot to create a lacquer.

Soften brown sugar by placing a slice of apple in the jar.

Check whether an egg is fresh by immersing it in a pan of cold water. If it sinks, it is fresh; if it rises to the surface, throw it away.

Remove food stains from your fingers by rubbing with sliced raw potato and rinsing with water.

Resting meat for half the time it has cooked will retain the juices and ensure it is tender and evenly coloured.

It is easier to thinly slice meat such as prosciutto, pancetta or carpaccio if it is partially frozen.

When storing cut melons or pumpkins, scoop out the seeds and stuff balls of paper towel in the cavities to absorb any excess juice.

Remove the skin from garlic easily by either crushing or microwaving for 15 seconds first.

When toasting whole seeds, soak them in water for 5 minutes, drain and toast in a sauté pan until fragrant.

Where possible, buy whole spices and grind them in a portable coffee grinder. The flavour is so much better than in powdered spices.

Season food with cooked pepper by filling the pepper mill with toasted peppercorns.

Intensify the flavour of a dessert by adding salt to the ingredients.

Don't chop fresh herbs too finely or they will break down and the flavour will change.

Cut soft herbs backwards to prevent them from turning grey.

Store popcorn kernels in the freezer to encourage more kernels to pop.

When measuring rice, 1 cup of uncooked long-grain white rice makes 3 cups cooked.

Sharpen kitchen scissors by cutting a piece of steel wool.

Prevent fish fillets from sticking and stewing when pan-frying by patting them dry before cooking.

Soak wooden skewers or disposable chopsticks in water for 30 minutes so they won't burn during cooking.

When blind baking pastry, first roll it out between sheets of cling film with a little flour, place into a tin and blind bake with the cling film, not baking paper. Baking paper tends to crinkle and not hug the walls of the pastry. The plastic will not melt as long as there are sufficient baking beans.

If you forget to use a timer when baking a cake, a good way to tell if it is nearly ready is when you can smell it.

When boiling potatoes for mashing, add salt to the water to help the mashing process; when cooking potatoes to keep their shape, do not add salt to the water.

Index